Storybook Travels

Storybook Travels

From Eloise's New York to
Harry Potter's London ,
Visits to **30** of the Best-L♡ved
Landmarks in Children's Literature

COLLEEN DUNN BATES

& and

SUSAN LATEMPA

 TH   3 1901 03066 5121   NEW YORK

Published by Three Rivers Press, New York, New York.
Member of the Crown Publishing Group, a division of Random House, Inc.
www.randomhouse.com

THREE RIVERS PRESS and the Tugboat design are registered trademarks
of Random House, Inc.

Anne of Green Gables, Green Gables House, and other indicia of "Anne"
are trademarks and Canadian official marks of the Anne of Green Gables
Licensing Authority, Inc., used under license by Three Rivers Press.
Excerpts from *Anne of Green Gables* are used with permission of David
Macdonald, trustee, and Ruth Macdonald. *L. M. Montgomery* and other
names and images created by L. M. Montgomery are trademarks of
Heirs of L. M. Montgomery Inc.

Printed in the United States of America

DESIGN BY BARBARA STURMAN

Library of Congress Cataloging-in-Publication Data
is available on request.

ISBN 0-609-80779-X

10 9 8 7 6 5 4 3 2 1

First Edition

♡

This book is dedicated to (and wouldn't
have been possible without) our patient
and loving husbands, Darryl Bates and Dan
Milder, and to the women who introduced
us to both children's literature and travel:
our mothers, Ellie Dunn and Patricia Taylor.

Acknowledgments

We were lucky to have had many enthusiastic advisors as we researched this book, as well as invaluable assistance from family, friends, and tourism professionals.

First, thanks go to our fellow family traveler, Mitch Kaplan, for consulting on destinations and for his research and writing contributions. Thanks also to Jeff Book for sharing his research and Kathy Compagnon for sharing her Paris.

Thank you to the tourism media representatives in many of the storybook locations: Faye Bleigh and Susan Stark, Hannibal CVB; Lorraine Geiger, Taos CVB; Carol Horne, Tourism PEI; Richard Griffith, Air Canada; Brigitta Kroon-Fiorita, Netherlands Board of Tourism; Daniel Haberli, Graubunden Vacations; Evelyn Mock, Swiss Tourism; Lindsa Okada, Swissair; Janis Flippen, Ventura CVB; Helga Brenner-Kahn, German National Tourism Office; Michael Boyer, Hameln Marketing and Tourism; Vickie Ashford, Birmingham CVB; Kas Maglaris, Rubenstein Associates (The Plaza Hotel); Allison Grand, the itsy-bitsy Entertainment Co.; and Laurie Armstrong, San Francisco CVB.

Thanks to our advisors at our favorite local bookstores: Lise Friedman at Dutton's and Linda Urban at Vroman's.

A heartfelt thank you to the children's-book lovers and storybook-traveling families who gave us so many ideas and so much enthusiasm and support. They include Melinda Grubbauer, Anne Schiller, Barbara McKinzie-Slater, Jennifer, Jim, and Todd Barry, Michelle, Jim, Garret, and Nora Lang, (Colleen's) uncle Frank Purcell, Mark Shepard, and Juliet Blake.

And thanks are due to Susan Dietz, our friend, cheerleader, and producer; to Sally Pfeiffer, our website designer; to Betsy Amster, our agent; to Barbara Sturman, the book's designer; and to Carrie Thornton and Becky Cabaza, our editors. Thanks also to Robert Landau for the photographs and to Jill Ganon for the proposal editing and inspiration.

Thanks, above all, to our families: Dan, Patricia, and Irene Milder and Darryl, Erin, and Emily Bates, who made our storybook travels a joy.

Finally, we honor the memory of Lynn Angell, friend, advisor, and children's librarian, who once made her husband, Dave, drive 600 miles out of their way so she could see Pa's fiddle at Laura Ingalls Wilder's house.

Contents

will give children the flavor of Alec's exciting secret midnight rides on the wild black stallion that saved his life.

From the Mixed-up Files of Mrs. Basil E. Frankweiler (1967) BY E. L. KONIGSBURG

✈ *Destination: The Metropolitan Museum of Art, New York City*

When Claudia runs away from home, she does it in style, inviting her younger brother along and selecting the Metropolitan Museum for their new home. Their live-in adventures enliven Renaissance beds, Egyptian tombs, and medieval armor halls for young reader-visitors.

Hans Brinker or the Silver Skates (1865) BY MARY MAPES DODGE

✈ *Destination: Haarlem, Amsterdam, and Nearby Villages, the Netherlands*

Seldom has a country been as carefully and fully detailed in fiction for the young reader as in this quaintly entertaining book, whose young characters skate through a landscape of windmills, villages, churches, and canals—a landscape that is preserved today in Holland's open-air museums.

MORE DUTCH TREATS, 99

Harry Potter and the Sorcerer's Stone (1998) & Other Titles BY J. K. ROWLING

✈ *Destination: London, Windsor, and Durham, England*

A child's tour of London, nearby Windsor, and the northern city of Durham will gain richness and a bit of mystery with some Harry Potter sleuthing. Search for Platform 9¾ at King's Cross Station, and get a feel for Hogwarts on a tour of Eton, the historic boarding school, or on a visit to magnificent Durham Cathedral, which served as Hogwarts in the feature film.

THE AUDIBLE HARRY, 103

Heidi (1880) BY JOHANNA SPYRI   109

✈ *Destination: Graubünden, Switzerland*

A footpath up the mountain leads from a please-touch Heidi museum to a high mountain hut not unlike Alm Uncle's in the Swiss region of Graubünden, where Spyri lived and set her heartfelt tale.

Hill of Fire (1971) BY THOMAS P. LEWIS;
Illustrated by JOAN SANDIN   121

✈ *Destination: Paracutín Volcano, Michoacán, Mexico*

This easy-reader novel about a young Mexican boy's amazing experience as a witness to the birth of a volcano is based on a true story. Visitors to the volcano, Paracutín, can see the ruins of the church and easily imagine Pablo's surprise in the village where nothing had ever happened before.

Island of the Blue Dolphins (1960)
BY SCOTT O'DELL   127

✈ *Destination: Channel Islands National Park, Ventura/Santa Barbara, California*

Present-day visitors to the islands where Karana the Indian girl lived alone for eighteen years will find themselves on a wonderful boat and walking trip through a wildlife preserve where they'll be surrounded by the birds, otters, and dolphins she turned to for companionship.

ABOUT THE CHANNEL ISLANDS, 129

Kidnapped (1886) BY ROBERT LOUIS STEVENSON   135

✈ *Destination: Isle of Mull, Scotland*

Although it's now linked by ferry to the mainland, the Isle

of Mull still conveys the awe-inspiring isolation that awaited the kidnapped, shipwrecked young hero who landed there in Stevenson's adventure story.

MORE JOURNEYS ON THE *KIDNAPPED* ROUTE, 142

loved today. Pay tribute to this tale of plucky determination in the face of "progress" with a visit to Fort Washington Park (in the shadow of the great gray George Washington Bridge on the Hudson River) and a tour of the historic lighthouse.

TAR BEACH AND THE GREAT GRAY BRIDGE, 169

Little Women (1868) by Louisa May Alcott 171

✕ *Destination: Concord, Massachusetts*

The rare author's house that is meaningful for kids, Orchard House contains Louisa's desk, the costume trunk she and her sisters used for their "theatricals," and a room in which her artist sister May literally drew on the walls.

PLAN AHEAD FOR PROGRAMS, 175

HENRY HIKES TO FITCHBURG, 178

Madeline (1939) & Other Titles
by Ludwig Bemelmans 181

✕ *Destination: Paris, France*

Join Madeline on a walk across the Pont Neuf (but don't fall in like she did!), a visit to Notre Dame, and a dog search through the Tuileries and under the tables of Les Deux Magots. You just might find the "old house in Paris that was covered with vines."

MADELINE ON FILM AND DISK, 185

Make Way for Ducklings (1941)
by Robert McCloskey 189

✕ *Destination: Boston, Massachusetts*

Not only do real ducks and swan boats ply the Public Garden lake shown in this beloved picture book, but there's also a series of statues honoring the storybook duck family that settled there. Walking the ducklings' route serves as a perfect child-size introduction to Boston.

Maybelle the Cable Car (1952)

✈ *Destination: San Francisco, California*

Nothing captivates young San Francisco visitors more than a ride on a cable car, so make the experience even more meaningful by reading about the travails of Maybelle and viewing the giant underground pulleys and wheels at the Cable Car Museum.

Paddle-to-the-Sea (1941)

✈ *Destination: Niagara Falls, Ontario, Canada*

With this beautifully illustrated, award-winning book about a canoe carved by an Indian boy in hand, a trip to Niagara Falls and a ride on a MAID OF THE MISTS boat to the foot of the falls is especially memorable.

The Pied Piper of Hamelin (1888)

✈ *Destination: Hamelin, Germany*

Several authors, including the great English poet Robert Browning, were inspired by the legend of Hamelin's mysterious medieval tragedy. This makes Hamelin, a rare intact Renaissance-era town with summertime Pied Piper pageants, a key point on the family-travel map.

you'll be accompanied by young Kenneth Watson, the fictional boy who visits his grandmother's neighborhood during the turbulent, historic weeks of September, 1963.

✈ *Destination: Chicago, Illinois*
Share smart, sassy Yolonda's love of Chicago with a trip to the annual Blues Festival in Grant Park, where she schemes to show the world that her little brother, a quiet boy who can't (won't?) learn to read, is a musical genius. The stars at the book's climax—B.B. King, John Hammond, Koko Taylor—could very well be playing at next summer's festival.

Our collection of thirty storybook travels is a fine beginning—and here are some more wonderful children's books with real-world settings.

Storybook
Travels

Introduction

Nothing could rob her of her birthright of fancy or her ideal world of dreams. And there was always the bend in the road!

—From *Anne of Green Gables*, by Lucy Maud Montgomery

The world first opens up to children in the pages of great books, taking them in their imaginations to fascinating places near and far: a farmhouse on Prince Edward Island, a cave on the banks of the Mississippi River, a long-ago village in Holland, a convent school in Paris, a fancy hotel in New York City. When children travel into the wide world this way, in their minds, they are traveling with some of the most enthralling companions they'll ever meet: Anne of Green Gables, Tom Sawyer, Jo March, Hans Brinker, Paddington Bear, Henry Huggins, Madeline, and their literary peers.

Sometimes, of course, the geography of children's literature is fantastical. Only Dorothy can really visit Oz, and we have looked in vain for Willy Wonka's chocolate factory and the territorial boundaries of Digitopolis.

But often the worlds described in children's literature are quite real. Many an author has drawn inspiration from the actual landscape of his or her youth—think of Louisa May Alcott, Mark Twain, and Beverly Cleary. Other writers have created memorable, even definitive portraits of a place by telling a story that communicates the setting's uniqueness, as Christina Bjork does in *Linnea in Monet's Garden,* or by inventing a character who couldn't come to life anywhere else, as Laurence Yep does in *Child of the Owl.*

These actual places, so vividly imagined by young readers and so fondly remembered by adults, can become the scenes of real-life adventures. Great stories transport the reader, in his or her imagination, to another place. So why not go there for real?

In the Footsteps of Great Books

If you've ever finished the last page of a really good book and wished you could see for yourself what the author described, or closed your eyes after reading a poem and dreamed of standing where the poet stood, you're not alone. Travelers in medieval Japan, Victorian England, and 1950s America have all taken to the road clutching a volume by Narihira, Boswell, or Kerouac. The charms of a modern city or the pleasures of a tropical paradise are enhanced for many tourists by the literary companionship of, for example, Hemingway in Paris or Twain in Hawaii.

And so it is with children and former children. *Storybook Travels* came about because we love to read with our children and travel with them, just as we loved being read to and taken places when we were kids. We decided to combine those pleasures and began searching out the settings of some great children's books to see what was really out there.

What wonderful discoveries awaited us! Children's literature has been growing in importance and quality in the past hundred years, entering a golden age in the last half of the twentieth century. Not surprisingly, it turns out that many of the finest works of children's literature are blessed with real-life settings. But less obviously, it also turns out that many of these settings are eminently worth traveling to—indeed, some are located at or near some of the most popular travel destinations in the world: Tuscany, the Grand Canyon, San Francisco's Chinatown, the Lake District of England, the California coast, New York City, and so on.

And, happily, we have found that interest in and preservation of the landmarks of children's literature is running high. Some settings are, in fact, more fun to visit with children now than they would have been a dozen years ago. The farmhouse described in *Anne of Green Gables*, for example, is now a Canadian national park, and it offers activities and games that show kids about farm life at the turn of the century. Some of the historic *Little House on the Prairie* homesteads not only have been preserved but more recently have begun sponsoring living-history events that allow kids to see the prairie from under a bonnet's brim. In Birmingham, Alabama, a visit to the new Civil Rights Institute offers perspective and understanding for the young reader of *The Watsons Go to Birmingham—1963* that would be impossible for parents alone to provide.

What Makes a Storybook Travel?

Between us, we journeyed to the settings of dozens of children's books in North America and Europe. We narrowed our favorites down to thirty and devoted one chapter of *Storybook Travels* to each title, arranged alphabetically, from *The Adventures of Pinocchio* to *Yolonda's Genius*. In lively conversations about these and many other books, we debated literary quality, the possible fun of a family trip to a setting, geographic balance, and other concerns.

In the end, our criteria were straightforward. We included

only fiction—storybooks—that we liked and, more importantly, that at least one of our kids or friends' kids liked. We chose books aimed at the 3- to 13-year-old child, with a particular emphasis on titles to be read to, by, or with kids from kindergarten to early middle school. Whether the book was published last year or 150 years ago, we wanted to be sure it was widely read today, so we looked for books that are on school reading lists, have won Newbery or Caldecott awards, and/or are strong sellers. (Many books are all three!) We looked for both classics and more current tales, and we set aside (for now) fairy tales, such as the Hans Christian Andersen stories, and tales of legendary figures, such as Paul Bunyan and Robin Hood.

As mothers who are also travel writers, we are sensitive to the practicalities of turning a family vacation into a literary pilgrimage. We feel that in order to recommend book settings as travel destinations, a place should offer not only the possibility of in some way re-creating the fictional character's experiences, but also a decent choice of such traditional vacation pursuits as swimming, museum-going, and sight-seeing. And as mothers, we know that adult-style literary pilgrimages—trooping through authors' birthplaces, for instance—are torture for most kids. Our goal is to thoroughly engage children in experiences that link to the books—to say "Charge it, please," at the Plaza, as Eloise did, or to walk the ducklings' walk just like in *Make Way for Ducklings*.

The travels we undertook to research this book were spread out over a few years. Our kids' ages are given as their ages at the time of the trip. (Colleen's daughters are Emily and Erin, Susan's are Patricia and Irene.) We also traveled with relatives and friends and the children of relatives and friends, and once in a while we even hooked up with school field-trip groups. In addition, we interviewed kids on the spot and got their unvarnished opinions.

What About . . . ?

As we researched *Storybook Travels*, we read and reread many wonderful children's books that have a real place as a setting. In order to share some of what we learned about additional books, we've added brief descriptions of another dozen or so titles in some chapters. These sidebars might describe other titles by the same author or other stories with similar settings. They are mentioned by theme in the table of contents, and you can find the individual titles in the index of titles on page 261.

But some titles, for one reason or another, didn't end up as chapters. We've gathered these books into a reading list called "More Storybook Travels," found on page 257. We haven't yet made it to many of the places described in those volumes, and if you get there before we do, we'd love to hear about it. Contact us at info@storybooktravels.com and give us the lowdown on *your* memorable storybook travels.

The Traveling Family

*Some Things to Keep in Mind When Planning a
Storybook Travel—or Any Vacation—with Children*

From time to time, we have seriously questioned
the wisdom of traveling with children. We remember the time, for instance, that one daughter, then five, threw up all over the carefully chosen stash of toys, snacks, and audiotapes at the beginning of a long road trip. Or the time another child, then seven, became panicky about San Francisco's traffic and noise and refused to walk another step, convinced we were all going to be hit by a runaway taxi. Or the time a nine-year-old daughter dismissed her French grilled-cheese sandwich as "disgusting" and then whined with hunger for hours.

No one knows more than we do how challenging family travel can be. But no one knows more than we do how great are its rewards. Over the years, we have been fortunate enough to take regular breaks from daily life to roam North America and Europe with our families. The original motivation may have been more selfish than we'd like to admit—*"I'm not going to let having a child stop me from going to Paris!"*—but the results have been more rewarding than we could ever have imagined.

Yes, children are most content when they are in the groove of a comfortable routine. But we've watched our children become happier and infinitely more mature as we have taken the trouble to shake up those routines. The once food-phobic child now has confidence that she will find something palatable (perhaps even delicious!) to eat wherever she goes. The once-shy early adolescent now feels at ease with everyone from a California park ranger to an Italian kid who speaks only ten words of English. The structure-obsessed child has learned not to fall apart when plans change unexpectedly.

But we don't mean to suggest that you can or should travel with kids exactly the same way you'd travel with other adults. If you hope for them to have a memorable experience—and for you not to go insane—you'll plan a trip with these five guidelines in mind:

1. **Less Is More Than Enough.** Perhaps when you were in college you managed to cram the Eiffel Tower, the Louvre, Notre Dame, and the Tuileries into one fun-filled Paris day. Don't even think of trying it with children. Limit yourself to one big outing a day with young children, maybe two with older kids.

2. **Have a Focus.** That's where *Storybook Travels* comes in. A day of aimless museum wandering can alienate a child in a hurry. But a trip to New York's Metropolitan Museum after reading *From the Mixed-up Files of Mrs. Basil E. Frankweiler* will be a wonderful adventure. When you set out with a mission that kids can get behind, everybody's likely to end up satisfied at the end of the day.

3. **Give Kids a Voice.** This is true whether your child is four or fourteen, although you wouldn't give a 4-year-old's voice the same weight as a 14-year-old's. For little kids, letting them decide between whether you'll take the bus or subway is plenty. Older kids can take a much more active role in planning and executing a trip. When they have a say in the decision-making, children are much more likely to engage in the travel experiences.

4. **Keep Some Semblance of Routine.** Even if you're sleeping in a different hotel every night, you can preserve just enough of the routines that keep kids from falling apart. If your little one always has a nap after lunch, find a way to make that happen, even if it's a nap in the car while you drive. If your grade-schooler expects a snack at 3:30, honor that expectation. And respect the comfort item—a trip away from home is not the time to wean a child from a beloved blankie.

5. **Encourage Record-Keeping.** It isn't always easy, but it's worth the effort. Equip each child with a journal, a pen, and a glue stick, and set aside a little time every day for the journals. Let them decide how to fill the journal—some may draw, some may write, and some may glue in pictures, ticket stubs, and other mementos; many will do all three. The act of recording helps them process their experiences, and when memories begin to fade, a year or two later, they will treasure their journals, even if they complained about having to make them at the time.

The Adventures of Pinocchio (1883)

BY CARLO COLLODI

Collodi, Tuscany, Italy

Tuscany is a well-known A-list destination for traveling grown-ups—but not many people know that because of the tiny village of Collodi it's also a wonderful place to take children. In the 1950s, the proud residents of Collodi built Parco di Pinocchio to honor native son Carlo Lorenzini, the author of Italy's most beloved children's book, who used his village's name for his pen name. For children (and adults) who have read the original book, Parco di Pinocchio makes an excellent day's outing.   —CDB

This trip is ideal for families with readers between the ages of 9 and 12, although even toddlers will enjoy the park.

The Book

Forget the Disney movie—Pinocchio is no adorable, cherub-faced moppet. Born in 1881, when the first in a series of Italian newspaper-serial chapters was published, he is a lanky, sharp-featured marionette carved out of a magic piece of wood by Geppetto, who is not a kindly toymaker but an old man known in the village for his silly yellow wig and his fierce temper. From the first instant, Pinocchio is a wild little monster, beginning life by kicking his new father, running away, and inadvertently getting Geppetto jailed for child abuse.

And don't expect to get the warm fuzzies from Jiminy Cricket. Called the Talking Cricket in the book, he so annoys Pinocchio with his advice that in the first few pages, the impulsive puppet hurls a hammer at the cricket and kills him.

The surprise was how much our kids, who've seen the Disney movie about a thousand times, enjoyed the book. True, it has many of the same characters and plot lines as the film: Pinocchio is misled by the thieving Fox and Cat, runs off to the Land of the Toys (Pleasure Island in the movie), is turned into a donkey, and is swallowed by a giant shark (a whale in the movie), in whose belly he is reunited with his father. And at the end, of course, he becomes a real boy.

But the book describes (and sometimes satirizes) the rough life of Italian village peasants more than a hundred years ago, a life that seems unimaginable to today's pampered American kids. People are thrown in jail often and for little reason. Brawls, fistfights, and beatings are common. And children are expected to dote on and eventually provide for their parents, not the other way around. In fact, what finally makes Pinocchio a real boy, and a success in life, is not his schooling or work but the fact that he takes care of his aging parents (by the end the Azure Fairy has become his mother figure).

Perhaps those differences add to the book's appeal for modern kids. Or, more likely, the sheer fancifulness of the story is what really captivates them. Pinocchio and Geppetto may be humble peasants, but their lives are full of magic and hair-raising adventure. In true serial fashion, every chapter details some close call, chase, fight, or reconciliation. The marionette nearly loses his life at least six times and gets into countless scrapes, typically vowing to return to school and be a good boy after each mishap. But because growing up doesn't happen overnight, it takes Pinocchio thirty-six chapters and lots of trial and error to become worthy of being a real boy. Take note that there are many, many editions of this book. Try to find an unabridged version, which is much richer in adventure and detail. If you can't find one in the United States, just wait until you arrive in Italy. Just about every bookstore and souvenir shop in Tuscany sells English-language versions of the unabridged story.

The Experience

Although our research had uncovered next to nothing on Parco di Pinocchio (it's almost never mentioned in English-language guidebooks), we parents knew not to expect Disney-style rides and multimedia showmanship. An American-style theme park just wouldn't make sense in this landscape of rolling forests, tidy vineyards, and Renaissance-era hilltop villages. Sure enough, Parco di Pinocchio was exactly what we grown-ups expected, a culturally uplifting place created by adults in the 1950s to honor the book, using bronze sculptures, mosaics, and other artwork created by the leading artists of the era. There wasn't a single ride or video game. And yet the kids adored it.

Because they'd read the book in the days immediately preceding our outing (Erin, 10, read it on her own, and we parents read it aloud to 7-year-old Emily), the characters and stories were fresh in their minds. They raced joyfully through the gardens, stopping first at the puppet show in progress. The Italian dialogue soon sent Emily wandering to the neighboring playground to swing and climb, but her older sister was able to figure out the gist of the story from the puppets' behavior, the inflections, and the few words she could understand. She enjoyed the challenge and was pleased with herself for being so international.

Next they ran into the mosaic square, whose tiled walls tell the story of Pinocchio in pictures. They picked out the main characters and events, then continued on into the maze-like garden, the heart of the park. Around each bend was a surprise. My daughters were most enchanted with the House of the Blue Fairy, a dollhouse-like structure with prismatic windows allowing glimpses into shimmering blue "rooms." Emily decided right then and there to be the Blue Fairy for the next Halloween. But their favorite feature was the huge shark's mouth (which looks more like a whale's). It's the most interactive of the sculptures—stepping-stones across water took them into its gaping mouth, and a spiral staircase took them atop his head, from which water shot forth regularly. They loved it.

Running along the garden paths with them, and getting lost in the labyrinth next to them, were kids and parents from all over: a couple of Americans, a few more Brits, some Italians, and a mix of French, Germans, Belgians, and other Europeans. But their numbers were relatively few—the sculptures seemed as plentiful as the people. Crowds are clearly not an issue here.

The Itinerary

An outing to Parco di Pinocchio can take a couple of hours or a whole day, depending on where your Tuscan starting point is. If you're staying north of Florence—say, in Lucca, a wonderful sixteenth-century walled town with fairy-tale appeal—the park should be a fairly quick drive, perhaps twenty minutes. If you're staying south of Florence, as we did, you'll have a longer drive and Florence traffic to contend with. On the map it didn't seem far from our tiny Chianti village to the equally tiny village of Collodi, but the combination of stop-and-go country roads and *autostrada* bottlenecks resulted in a two-hour drive each way. Although it is significant to Italians, the park is low-key by

American theme-park standards, and it's not exactly on anyone's beaten path. From the A11 *autostrada*, take the Chiesina U. exit and follow the many (but small) signs that will lead you to the park via the midsize town of Pescia.

If you're hungry, consider stopping in Pescia, where there are many more choices than in Collodi. We were quite pleased with the pizza at Del Magro, a plain little bar/café where the four of us had pizza and Pellegrino for only $10; several other nearby restaurants looked worthy. Or allow time for a sit-down meal at Osteria del Gambero Rosso (House of the Red Shrimp), Parco di Pinocchio's adjacent restaurant. Or, perhaps best of all if the weather's fine, pick up picnic fare in Pescia and have lunch at one of the many tables in the park.

As you enter the ancient hillside village of Collodi, you'll see a grand building on the hillside to your right. Called Giardino Villa Garzoni, this fanciful castle is known for its ornate eighteenth-century terraced gardens, complete with strange topiary, statues of mythical beasts, and water staircases. If you have time, stop here for a spell; because of its eccentricity, it's far more interesting to kids than most gardens.

A little further on lies Parco di Pinocchio. Outside the park's gate (manned by one sleepy ticket seller) is a row of souvenir stands. Skip these and head into the park, whose own shop is a little better. Once you're through the gate, pathways will guide you through the property: past Emilio Greco's sculpture *Pinocchio and the Fairy*, through the outdoor puppet theater and the mosaic piazza (created by Venturino Venturi), to the giant chessboard, and into the garden maze. The kids can race ahead on the paths and make the discoveries: the House of the Blue Fairy, statues of the book's many characters (the Assassins, the Crab, the Blue Fairy, Pinocchio, the Serpent), the aforementioned Giant Shark, a cool underground pirate's cave (although there are no pirates in the book), some immobile boats on water, whose connection to the book are mysterious, and a mock village that unsuccessfully attempts to remind kids of Pinocchio's village. Behind the Giant Shark is a labyrinth that's fun to brave.

Parco di Pinocchio is a small place, and high-energy kids could whip through the whole place in forty-five minutes. But encourage them to slow down. Try watching the puppet show, even if the language is a mystery. Hang around the playground for a while. Linger over a game of giant chess. Stop in the little café/souvenir shop for an ice cream and a wooden Pinocchio doll. And make sure to allow time to browse in the museum–library center. Our whole family found the collection of Pinocchio-related toys, dolls, movie posters, and books fascinating (yes, Disney is well represented here). After seeing the exhibits, along with several academic treatises on the significance of Pinocchio to Italy's national identity, we began to understand the cultural significance of the little wooden boy.

Names and Numbers

Parco di Pinocchio
Collodi, Tuscany
(39) (0572) 429342
www.pinocchio.it
Open daily 8:30 A.M.–sunset

Osteria del Gambero Rosso
Adjacent to Parco di
    Pinocchio
(39) (0572) 429364

Giardino Villa Garzoni
Collodi, Tuscany
Open daily 9 A.M.–5 P.M.
(39) (0572) 429590

The Adventures of Tom Sawyer (1876)

BY MARK TWAIN

Hannibal, Missouri, and Environs

Although *The Adventures of Tom Sawyer* depicts an era more than 150 years in the past, it's still possible, in the very town where Twain grew up and set this all-American boyhood story, to camp on Jackson Island, explore a limestone cave, hunt for mushrooms in the woods . . . and hear many a tall tale. —SLT

This trip is ideal for families with readers between the ages of 8 and 13, as well as younger and older siblings.

The Book

This Mark Twain favorite is so familiar, you think it's going to make dull reading: Tom Sawyer whitewashing the fence, falling in love with Becky Thatcher, heading with a dead cat and Huck Finn to the cemetery at midnight, hiding out with Huck and Joe Harper on Jackson Island. We've seen Disney versions and cartoon versions. We've read parodies and homages. Yeah, yeah, we know: It's important American literature—Tom Sawyer's pre–Civil War adventures provide a snapshot of the lives of Americans uniquely poised at the moment of the western expansion. Twain's images of life on the Mississippi River are an indelible part of the American consciousness. His use of vernacular was a literary breakthrough, and his popularity as an author is itself a page in history. All this bodes well for the classroom—but what about reading just for fun?

Well, it's impossible to predict any one child's reactions, but a moderately capable adult reading out loud ought to be able to hold an elementary-school-age listener's attention with *The Adventures of Tom Sawyer* as easily as with a campfire ghost story. And the prose is quite accessible, so families who have the tradition of the parent and child taking turns reading aloud from the same book will find this an excellent choice. The dialogue is superb, allowing for exciting dramatization. Twain's narrative voice is pointed and persuasive, so the story moves along rapidly from scene to scene. His characters—orphans, slaves, abused children—give us an unsentimental record of a rough world, but they are sturdy and resourceful in colorful and often humorous situations. Overall, *The Adventures of Tom Sawyer* reflects the optimism that is a hallmark of our national character.

And the setting is one of the most memorable aspects of the book. Readers young and old will see vivid mental pictures as they read: the Mississippi River, the sandbar off Jackson Island, the endless maze of the cave, and the buildings—schoolhouse, hilltop mansion, tavern—that make up the nineteenth-century town. These aren't empty landscapes, but rather are populated with kids—Tom, Becky, Huck, Joe, Sid, and other characters—sneaking out of the house at midnight, floating on a log raft, picnicking under oak trees, smoking corncob pipes, prowling around haunted houses, and getting themselves lost in a spooky, dark cavern.

The Experience

During our trip to Hannibal, sixth-graders were gathered around the cave guide, Mike, a plain-spoken, deadpanning veteran of many a school group visit.

"Now, don't go wandering down passageways that branch out from our trail," he warned the students. "There's one part of the cave where we used to keep a dead body."

"Can we see the dead body?" a voice immediately piped up.

"And we have bats in here, remember. They usually don't bother us, but another reason to stay with the group is that the bats have been known to dive-bomb people who are alone."

"*Yes!*" exulted one of the listening boys. There was nothing he wanted more than to be dive-bombed by a bat.

"Now from time to time," Mike continued, "I'll be turning lights on and off. If I accidentally plunge us into total darkness, the appropriate thing to do is . . . *scream!*"

On that note, and as Mike turned to lead us into Mark Twain's Cave, the kids began to practice their screams, the sounds echoing enthusiastically off the limestone walls of the oldest show cave (a cave open to the public for touring) in Missouri.

We were on a swing through the Midwest, visiting friends and relatives, when we decided to tag along with a friend who'd volunteered to accompany her son's sixth-grade class on an overnight field trip to Hannibal. The kids had read *The Adventures of Tom Sawyer* in class, seen one of the several videos, and were by now pretty blasé about Tom, Becky, Huck, and Joe.

But it turned out that Hannibal was cool. Oh, sure, they would have to walk through a small museum later that day, but they'd begun their visit the day before with a riverboat ride highlighted by several excruciatingly loud blasts of the steam whistle. The pilot had warned the passengers that the sound would actually be painful for those folks sitting right in front of the bridge, so a half dozen of the boys had immediately run to that location and waited expectantly for the experience. (They were not disappointed, yowling in agony when the whistle blew.) For supper, they'd picnicked in a park on a high bluff overlooking the Mississippi River, so there were plenty of chances to pretend that they were almost falling over the edge—down, down for miles. And because it was spring, the river was rising, so after dinner they got to walk on the levee and see how the town was behind a wall, and how maybe the whole place could flood in a few days. Then, on the last night, they camped at the campground right next to the cave, and one of their teachers made catfish for breakfast, cooking in an iron skillet over the fire. Even if you didn't like fish, it was cool because he left the head on and everything. And Tiffany saw a snake.

The Itinerary

Tom Sawyer and Huck Finn linger in the adult imagination as perpetual boys of summer, bare feet dangling in the Mississippi River as they fish and laze in the sun. That spirit of summer, that feeling of the long, slow days of a nineteenth-century boyhood (punctuated by adventure, to be sure), is the great gift parents can give their kids on a Tom Sawyer trip.

You could hasten into Hannibal on a hurried one-day stop and come away irritated by a small town's amateurish efforts to cash in on a famous son. It's possible to stay in a generic highway motel, tramp in and out of the gift shops in the historic district, and give the riverboat ride and the cave a pass, assuming you know what they'll be like, but that's not a good idea.

You'd miss tall tales told by local guides who have such an inborn understanding of Twain's rhythm and language that they seem to be quoting him when they're merely improvising. Who tell you, "We used to go down to the cave with a sandwich and a flashlight." Who say, "Ask us any question that comes to mind, and we'll be sure to make up an interesting answer for you." Who tell you where Tom Sawyer did this and where Huck Finn did that.

You'd miss the wonderful sight of a three-foot crane standing by the side of the road with an equally long black snake grasped in its beak. Or maybe you'd miss the kid-tourist thrill of "mining for gemstones" or playing miniature golf.

You'd miss, in the case of the riverboat, a lovingly refurbished and maintained craft piloted by a lifelong river buff. You'd miss not only the captain's kid-pleasing steam whistles, but the moment when he turns off the microphone and a hush descends as he suggests that everyone pretend they're on the river 150 years ago, hearing the birds and the wind in the trees as the boat moves slowly, majestically against the current of the wide Mississippi.

One way to slow things down is to take your time getting to Hannibal. From St. Louis, drive to Hannibal on Scenic Highway 79. The very moment you pull off Interstate 70, the urban world drops away and you're in a landscape of turf farms, barns, silos, and cow pastures. Lacking an adult's historical perspective, your kids probably won't be transported back a century as you drive along this road, but they will be in the country. On the way, you can check out some parts of the Mark Twain National Wildlife Refuge to learn about the Mississippi River plants, animals, and birds (from wild turkeys to woodpeckers) that Tom and Huck knew so well. We spotted the small, inconspicuous sign for the Clarence Cannon section of the reserve and drove five minutes off Highway 70 down a gravel road to a wetlands nature center with wildlife observation posts and bird-watching information (more than two hundred species are seen along this part of the river migration route). In season, staff will help visitors find areas for mushroom hunting and berry or nut picking. Another accessible stop is in the hamlet of Clarksville, where there's a small park and visitor center and an eagle lookout for glimpses of this magnificent bird.

In Hannibal, the must-do family experiences are the riverboat and the cave(s), commercial attractions that promise to re-create moments in the book: the riverboat ride to Becky's picnic and Tom and Becky's getting lost for days in the cave.

Boat trips leave from the downtown dock three times a day from May through Labor Day; the schedule varies in April, May, September, and October. Dinner cruises with musical entertainment might get everyone focused on sitting down and eating, so if you can take the afternoon ride, you'll be more likely to smile indulgently as the kids race from deck to deck. The late-night blues cruise appeals mainly to the cocktail crowd, but because of the many midnight scenes in *The Adventures of Tom Sawyer,* it might be a fun option with older kids on a moonlit night. If the water's right, the boat goes around the island that Twain calls Jackson Island, where you can still camp and swim as the boys did if you have a private boat (or can hire one) to get you there.

Mark Twain Cave, about a mile south of Hannibal, is "developed," meaning it has some paved paths and electric lights. One area has a few colored lights. But overall it is in a natural condition. It is, after all, a National Historic Landmark, and even its graffiti, which dates back to the early 1800s and includes signatures from such famous folks as Jesse James, is protected. The one-hour tour is fun and informative for elementary-school-age kids. Middle- and high-school kids will love the Cameron Cave tour, which begins at the same location and calls for participants to carry battery-operated lanterns. It's also on level pathways and easy to walk (there's no crawling through passageways), but because the cave isn't lit, it will feel more authentic to older kids. Both caves have tours daily from Memorial Day through Labor Day, and Mark Twain Cave is open year-round.

For overnight stays in Hannibal, the best family bet is camping. There are three campgrounds, two with swimming pools and fishing lakes and one in a parklike setting next to woods with nature trails. Otherwise, the nicest lodgings are bed-and-breakfast inns, but check carefully, because many do not accommodate kids under 12. Sawyer's Creek Fun Park is an enjoyable small amusement park and miniature golf area south of downtown that is a good bet for casual riverfront dining.

Hannibal's main tourist area is the historic district at the riverfront, where you'll find the riverboat ride and various Twain-era landmarks. Among the shops is a glassblower who demonstrates his art by making marbles (a nice souvenir) and a weaving shop with a little museum where spinning is demonstrated. Finally, spend some time up on the bluffs in Riverview Park, where you can picnic and take an easy nature trail two-thirds of a mile long.

Names and Numbers

Hannibal Convention and
 Visitors' Bureau
505 N. Third St.
Hannibal
(573) 221-2477,
(866) 263-4825
www.hanmo.com

Mark Twain Cave and
 Cameron Cave
1 mile south of Hannibal
 on Hwy. 79
(573) 221-1656
www.marktwaincave.com
(*Note that the walking path
is level and there are no steps,
but it is not wheelchair
accessible.*)

Mark Twain Riverboat
Center St. Landing
Hannibal
(573) 221-3222
fax (573) 221-5335
www.marktwainriverboat.com

Mark Twain National
  Wildlife Refuge
1704 N. 24th St.
Quincy, Illinois
(217) 224-8580

Clarence Cannon Site
Annada, Missouri
(573) 847-2333

And Now Miguel (1953)

BY JOSEPH KRUMGOLD

Taos, New Mexico

Much has changed in New Mexico's Rio Grande Valley since the early 1950s, when Joseph Krumgold, a documentary film-maker, first filmed and then fictionalized the daily life of the middle child of a sheepherding family. But the mesa, the mountains, and the rivers are unchanged, and—in a place where tradition is highly esteemed—there are many reminders of the region's tricultural past.

—SLT

This trip is ideal for families with readers between the ages of 10 and 12, and older siblings.

The Book

In 1953, when Krumgold published *And Now Miguel*, the word *multiculturalism* hadn't been compounded yet. This Newbery Award–winning novel, the story of 12-year-old Miguel Chavez, would have been a bit of exotica for most urban and suburban American kids. At the time, books mentioning characters' ethnic backgrounds focused on European immigrants.

But today, a half century later, Miguel lives on in this book, and his story—filled with colorful details by someone who closely observed the patterns and rhythms of a distinctive regional way of life—is testimony to a proud heritage. We now recognize him as an all-American boy, and he's the more cherished for being one of so few kid characters from that era to have been portrayed with specific cultural characteristics (which in Miguel's case include his bilingualism and his reverence for his village's patron saint).

Poised at the brink, he thinks, of manhood, Miguel shares with the reader his dreams and deep thoughts as he works to gain recognition from his father and other adults. His sphere of activity is at once tiny (a family home and a little village near Taos) and vast (the enormous valley that stretches to the horizon, where the Sangre de Cristo Mountains loom). It's Miguel's ambition to go into those mountains, to walk with the men when they drive the herd to high pastures and stay for three summer months at the sheep camps in the mountains. He begins at the New Year to try to show his father and grandfather how well he can work, how he's almost a man.

And Now Miguel (along with Krumgold's other Newbery-honored title, *Onion John*) is a book that sixth-graders are commonly assigned. Teachers will tell you it's a good book, and they're right, but what with questions to answer on every chapter and projects to do on the life cycle of a sheep, some kids lose enthusiasm for the story as the weeks of the required reading drag on. Still, many others will find themselves reading ahead as they get caught up in Miguel's dilemmas, and some, after reading of Miguel's longing, may look at their little brothers and sisters a bit differently when they finish the book. If you come into the room as your son is reading *Miguel* and he has a few tears in his eyes, you'll know that he shares some of the young hero's intense need to figure out the whys and wherefores of the adult world, when all he knows are the words and formulas of childhood.

This is a terrific book to share aloud with slightly younger kids, too, and everyone but experienced 4-H members will learn plenty from the passages detailing such events as the birth of a lamb, the pitiful orphaning of another lamb, the fascinating struggles to keep ewes and lambs together, and the intensity of shearing season. Each moment in the family's livestock-raising year, though, is seen through its emotional significance to Miguel, who sets himself a sort of labors-of-Hercules training course.

Does he make it into the mountains? Not without setbacks, not without anguish—but yes, triumphantly, Miguel goes into the mountains.

The Experience

Taos is a city that proudly embraces three major historic traditions (Native American, Hispanic, and Anglo frontier) as well as countless more recent identity groups. As my friend's son Danny and I strolled the retail areas of town, we noted signs of fierce loyalty to many ways of life—from the outdoor way of life to the potter's way of life, the Wiccan way of life to the tourist biz way of life. We saw and heard calls to arms from spiritual activists, culinary activists, art activists, environmental activists, and many others.

Although Danny, who is a little younger than Miguel, was most interested in the tattooed-teens-who-hang-around-the-central-plaza way of life, we were looking for sheep. Driving around (in the champagne-colored convertible Danny had convinced me to upgrade to at the rental counter), we had not only thrilled to the fragrant high-altitude air, but spotted *ranchitos* all around the outskirts of Taos, which is a compact city by western standards. At a few, we even saw small flocks of a dozen or so sheep.

But after a chat with the folks at Weaving Southwest, a shop and school, and at La Lana Wools, where Danny bought a soft toy lamb with a shank of real raw wool on its back for his little sister, and I bought some seductive plant-dyed wool felt squares, we learned that to see herds of "many hundreds" of sheep, as Miguel's family managed, we'd have to head to nearby Chama Valley. There a group of livestock growers, Ganados del Valle, has a cooperative breeding program to save the old Spanish Churro sheep line from extinction, and it has other programs to "ensure that weaving, wool growing, and sheepherding continue as a way of life."

But the sheep would have to wait a day or two, because our first order of business was a raft ride. Danny had first donned an orange life jacket for the rapids in Glenwood Springs, Colorado, and he had enjoyed a calm-water rafting excursion near the Grand Canyon. When we drove into Taos at the Rio Grande Gorge and saw rafters far below in a beautiful canyon setting, I agreed to sign up with an outfitter.

In the morning, we compromised on the length and thrill quotient of the ride and rafted through the Lower Gorge from the Orilla Verde Recreation Area south of town. There the Rio Grande, although its current still moves briskly, has smooth, grassy shores and pleasant picnic and camping sites. We were reminded of Miguel's weeks spent fishing (and sulking) in the book, and we talked to some anglers who said they hoped to catch trout (but not as Miguel did, with his hands) or pike. Our rafting trip took us twelve miles south through enough white water to satisfy Danny without making my hair stand on end.

That afternoon, after a terrific meal that included some of the foods Miguel describes ("a stew that was made to taste good with red chili" and *"sopaipillas,* a sort of a puffed-up kind of biscuits [that were] what Faustina liked best"), we went to Taos Pueblo. Miguel doesn't describe going into the pueblo itself, but rather talks about how his family rents land from the Indians for grazing. Still, the winter sheep camp would have been on the plateau right near the historic buildings, so we figured Miguel and his brother would have seen the pueblo's silhouette. After some hesitation, Danny and I decided to join a guide on one of the walking tours. The pueblo is haunting, with the familiar outlines of its four-hundred-year-old buildings rising three stories into the bright blue sky, but it seems small as you stand in the plaza, and it seemed awkward to walk around areas where people live. We were self-conscious about being tourists.

Happily, our guide made us feel comfortable, and we were genuinely pleased with her narration. Danny the more so because I'd already failed to know the answers to several of his questions ("When did they add doors?" "Are there people living in all of the apartments?" "How do they decide who gets to live here?" "Are they related to the people at San Idelfonso Pueblo, where we went yesterday?" "Where did they hang the chiefs after the revolt?").

With the endless energy of a preteen, Danny next proposed a drive into Miguel's beloved Sangre de Cristo Mountains, where (he'd read) there was a chairlift at Taos Ski Valley that operates even in the summer months.

We rose into the mountains on the lift, Danny swinging his feet and pointing, me trying to relax and not look down. Then at the top, my sense of self dropped away—as Miguel describes what had happened to him.

There was no more Miguel. Only a pair of eyes to look at the green, the great trees of pine and oak. Two eyes, and one nose to pull, like a lamb nursing, at how clean it was, and

sharp, to smell the chill that was here and the faraway soft
taste of the pine and the spruce.

The Itinerary

To see the world through Miguel Chavez's eyes, a family needs
to look at the Rio Grande Valley from both the grand, big-
picture visitor's view and the small, close-in resident's view.

First, we recommend plenty of outdoor activities, from
river rafting and hiking to a simple riverside picnic. In a general sense, you'll get an appreciation for the background of
Miguel's daily life and will remember passages in the book in
which he describes clouds as sheep or talks about being
caught in a rainstorm. Begin by pointing out similar features of
the landscape as you drive around: an adobe house under a
cottonwood tree like the one Miguel's older brother wants to
build; a small farmhouse with outbuildings.

The hamlet of Los Cordovas, where Miguel's father helps
build a chapel, is now an empty field surrounded by modest
rural homes, farm buildings, and trailers. It's not far from one
actual landmark that figures in the book: the San Francisco de
Asis Church in Ranchos de Taos, a massive adobe hulk familiar from Georgia O'Keeffe's painting of it, is "the big church in
Ranchos" mentioned several times.

A family trip shouldn't be about gazing out of car windows,
of course, so you'll want to get out into Miguel's world. Near
where Miguel's village was you'll find Hacienda de los Martinez, a history museum that preserves the buildings and
belongings of a Hispanic farming family that was richer and
from an earlier era than Miguel's. In spite of the differences, it
offers an introduction to the Spanish sheepherding tradition of
the region ("Long before there was any such thing here called

the United States, there was a Chavez family in this place with sheep," says Miguel), and you'll see displays of tools and furniture as well as sheepskins, looms, and other artifacts of this way of life. The Martinez Hacienda also exhibits an extraordinary collection of Northern New Mexican *santos*, or icons of saints (some with clothes that are changed with the seasons), which will help kids understand more about San Ysidro, who plays such an important role in Miguel's life.

A visit to the thousand-year-old Taos Pueblo will be a highlight of your trip and will weave in the thread of another great culture. The historic, walled part of the pueblo is operated by the Taos Pueblo tribal government (headed by an elected war chief, the official to whom Miguel's father paid pasture rent) as a combination sacred site and tourist attraction. Many rooms in the famous multistoried dwellings have been turned into art studios and shops, and visitors are invited in to watch artisans work and to purchase pottery, jewelry, and other art. Individual Native American concessionaires also sell bread baked in adobe ovens and offer horseback and sleigh rides.

Miguel's long trek across the mesa in search of a lost bunch of sheep can be the inspiration for a hike and a picnic. The West Rim Trail follows the Rio Grande River for nine miles. It can be accessed from the north at the spectacular gorge area, or from the south at Orilla Verde Recreation Area. There are also many beautiful day-use areas of the Kit Carson National Forest, where Miguel's family held a permit to graze sheep in the summer. The quickest and easiest access, just two miles from Taos's central plaza, is into Taos Canyon along U.S. 64, Paseo del Canyon Road, toward Angel Fire Ski Resort. You'll find some lovely picnic spots with tables under shady trees alongside the Rio Fernando, a small but lively stream.

Linger with some Northern New Mexico takeout of enchiladas and posole, and let the kids try to catch trout with their hands, as Miguel teaches his little brother to do.

To go into the Sangre de Cristo Mountains as Miguel did, drive along scenic Highway 150 into the Carson National Forest, where you can hike or ride horses, imagining that you're driving several hundred head of sheep as you go. Or, on the same route, visit the Taos Ski Valley for a chairlift ride. Either way, you'll pass the same peaks and landmarks that Miguel does.

Finally, if your visit is long enough, or you're coming in from southern Colorado, or your family includes train buffs, make plans for a day and an overnight in Chama, a town about two hours northwest of Taos. In Chama you'll find the western terminus of the Cumbres & Toltec Scenic Railroad, a remarkable restored narrow-gauge line running through the mountains between Chama and Antonito, Colorado. In summer and early fall, you can ride in vintage passenger cars into the mountains to an old stagecoach town for lunch, returning in late afternoon. There are several lodges and motels in Chama, most geared for fishing enthusiasts and situated along the river.

To or from the railroad excursion, *And Now Miguel* readers can stop at the picturesque historic village of Los Ojos, center of the wool-growing way of life. Here you'll find Tierra Wools, a weaver/spinner/grower-owned company that offers visitors a look at whatever activities are going on at the moment: raw wool washing, dyeing, and sorting. In a room with a dozen massive looms, women are sure to be weaving the beautiful tapestries and rugs exhibited and sold here. In the shop, you'll also find notecards by local photographer Dorothy Galloway depicting area sheepherders (some as young as Miguel) driving their flocks into the mountains. In the winter and early spring, the pastures around Los Ojos are home to large flocks of sheep.

Back in Taos, the annual Wool Festival is held in October

in a park in the middle of town. Weavers and wool-growers gather from around the world, and the public is invited for two days of shearing demonstrations, contests, workshops, vendor booths, and hands-on activities for kids.

Names and Numbers

Taos Visitor Center
1139 Paseo del Pueblo Sur
Taos
(800) 816-1516
www.taoschamber.com
www.taosguide.com

....

Taos Ski Valley Visitors' and
Convention Bureau
(800) 992-7669
www.taosskivalley.com

....

Bureau of Land
Management Taos
field office
(505) 758-8851
Rio Grande Gorge Visitor
Center
(505) 751-4899
*For information about the
West Rim Trail, Orilla Verde
Recreation Area, and other
outdoor recreation areas, as
well as a list of river-raft
outfitters.*

New Mexico Public Lands
Information Center
1474 Rodeo Rd.
Santa Fe
(505) 438-7542
www.publiclands.org
*For information about na-
tional forests (including Kit
Carson National Forest) and
state parks and wildlife areas.*

....

La Hacienda de los Martinez
Ranchitos Road
Taos
(505) 758-1000
www.taosmuseums.org

Taos Pueblo, a unesco
World Heritage Site
Taos Pueblo Tourism
(505) 758-1028
www.taospueblo.com
Open except during times of
religious observances; call
ahead to confirm openings.
Two main closures are Feb.–
Apr. for eight to twelve
weeks and late Aug.–early
Sept. for about ten days.

Weaving Southwest
216-B Paseo del Pueblo
Norte
Taos
(505) 758-0433

La Lana Wools
13 Paseo Norte
Taos
(505) 758-9631
www.lalanawools.com

La Tierra Wools
91 Main St.
Los Ojos
(505) 588-7231
(888) 709-0979
www.handweavers.com

Cumbres and Toltec Scenic
Railroad
Chama
(888) 286-2737
www.cumbrestoltec.com

Wool Festival
(888) 909-9665
www.taoswoolfestival.org

Anne of Green Gables (1908)
&and Other Titles

BY L. M. MONTGOMERY

Prince Edward Island, Canada

*F*ew books for young readers are imbued with as strong a sense of place as Lucy Maud Montgomery's atmospheric tales, eight altogether about Anne. Her red-haired heroine is not only a memorably mischief-prone youngster, but also a nature lover who frequently rhapsodizes about the beauty of the farmlands and woods. Today, almost a hundred years after this wonderful book first appeared, a pilgrimage to Anne's island is a satisfying journey to a place that is still very much as the author describes it. The highlight is Green Gables National Park—the only national park we know of that preserves the "home" of a fictional character.   —SLT

This trip is ideal for families with readers between the ages of 9 and 13, and their younger siblings will enjoy the fun, too.

The Books

In the early part of the twentieth century, a number of American and Canadian women were uniquely poised as authors. They themselves had received educations and might have traveled and developed wider worldviews, but they knew firsthand, from their own childhoods and from their mothers and grand-mothers, about the experiences of isolated rural folk. As we now see in their writing, these authors understood that women's roles were changing—they prepared the way for a new genera-tion of girls with tales of spunky, spirited heroines who didn't easily adapt to the narrow old ways of needlework, prayer, and the avoidance of worldly pleasure. In introducing these charac-ters, the writers also recorded the domestic details of the fading nineteenth century in such books for children as *Rebecca of Sunnybrook Farm* and *Understood Betsy*.

Thanks to being translated into seventeen languages, hav-ing been constantly in print, and spawning a successful stage musical and various movie and TV adaptations, *Anne of Green Gables* and its seven sequels are said to be the most globally known of these stories of girls in the olden days. No one, it seems, reads just one Anne book. The character is so appeal-ing, her voice so compelling, and the situations that she gets herself into (for she's no passive princess) so comical and/or horrifying that upon completing one volume, most readers straightaway begin on the next. True fans, having finished the Anne series, move on to books about Emily, Pat, and other Montgomery characters.

Anne's romantic nature and her heartfelt emotionalism are vividly portrayed as unique in an environment where hard work is a habit, source of pride, and reason for being, and where util-ity and thrift are admired above all. Her delighted responses to the beauties of nature—from the colors of a sunset to the fra-grance of garden flowers, from the changes of the season to the glories of a morning—are set down by the author as little mono-logues of exclamation. These prose poems spoken by the char-acter make the books different from many children's classics because they unite the young protagonist with the natural world, as well as with the people in it.

The Experience

When you consider a trip to Prince Edward Island (PEI), you may hear how hundreds of busloads of senior citizens and thousands of young Japanese women visit the Anne sites each year. Understandably, many people fear that the literary landmark has been commercialized and that PEI has been turned into a kind of Anne theme park.

But it just ain't so. What the islanders call "commercial development" (and work hard to contain and isolate) looks tasteful and quaint to anyone "from away." And for families, especially those with girls and boys between 8 and 12 who've read the books, the Anne sites really do offer images of the nineteenth century—never mind that fact and fiction are thoroughly blended. That's part of the charm.

"I came here because I love *Anne of Green Gables* so much," sighed a 10-year-old girl as we sat on a bench and gazed at the green-gabled house (once belonging to Montgomery's cousins) at Green Gables Prince Edward Island National Park.

"And because Dad promised," added her younger brother. "We come like once a year."

The two young PEI residents had, like many local children, previously visited Green Gables with school groups. They had learned from the docents about the details of life in Anne's day: about the "pee pots" in every room, and how ropes tied across the bedframes held up the mattresses. They had participated in activities such as ice cream making that illuminate pre-MTV lifestyles for young visitors.

The national park site consists of the Green Gables house,

furnished as if it were Marilla and Matthew's farmhouse, and some nature trails that duplicate settings described in the book (like the patch of trees that Anne calls the Haunted Wood). The park service recently added a barn, showing how the cows that Anne took care of would have been housed.

This low-tech, low-key world seems a paradise to many children. They're enthusiastic about the nature trails, especially the one with "rivers" that you can cross on little footbridges. Kids point out the trout in the streams and read the signs quoting passages from the books. Walking through the historic house (which looked to us adults much like ones that had been greeted in the past with yawns and irritation), they were often shouting out in recognition.

"Mom—look at the candle!"

"Julie—I think I see the strawberry cordial, but there's no currant wine."

"That's because Diana drank it, stupid."

One youngster earnestly checked with a docent about the mousetraps that should have been in the pantry (but weren't) and resolved to find them next time. Another thought the hair wreath was "cool" and asked if Anne was real. A very young child just wanted to touch the "gonkey" (donkey).

But adults can only guess at the appeal of being in Anne's world. As we went around the island and gazed into the shadows of the Haunted Wood, where Anne's imagination ran away with her, or looked at the bookcase where the author, like her heroine, had once made an imaginary friend out of the reflections in the glass, or sat down to tea in Charlottetown, as both author and character had done, or walked along the dunes at the beach at Cavendish, we could only be nostalgic. Watching the bright eyes of the girls of that special Anne-reading age between childhood and adolescence, we remembered the satisfying feeling that results when fiction and reality blend beautifully with the exercise of the imagination, and when the promise of an imagined future is built on the reality of today.

The Itinerary

Lucy Maud Montgomery grew up on Prince Edward Island and taught school here before moving to Ontario. The house that she visualized Anne living in is near the village of Cavendish, as was Montgomery's home, and this north-shore region, about an hour's drive from the main city of Charlottetown, is considered "Anne Country." A popular destination for summer family travel, the island is well supplied with housekeeping cottages near the beaches as well as campgrounds, hotels, and bed-and-breakfast inns. It's an idyllic site for several days of varied, often low key activities. Fans of the books will find details described by Anne everywhere, from red dirt roads and the historic Charlottetown Driving Park (a harness-racing track) to cow pastures and the seashore. Note that many attractions, restaurants, and hotels are open only in the summer, roughly May to October.

Visitors arrive both by car (over the Confederation Bridge or via ferry) and by plane. Charlottetown is roughly in the middle of the island. Depending on the ages of your kids and your family's enthusiasms, a good plan is to begin and end in Charlottetown. The stage version of *Anne of Green Gables,* presented there throughout the summer months, is a well-regarded summer-stock kind of show that will remind everyone of the flavor and fun of the books. A tearoom called Anne's Tea Party is a worthwhile stop. In an appropriately Victorian room (a chair rail, potted ferns), girls costumed as characters from the books serve an excellent cream tea, with scones made from Montgomery's recipe and the best strawberry preserves we've ever had.

A day or two on the north shore in the Cavendish area can include a farm stay, a strawberry-picking session, afternoons on the beach at PEI National Park, a calm-water kayaking or canoeing expedition departing from the beautiful fishing village of Rustico, and visits to Green Gables and other historic houses associated with Montgomery.

The Anne of Green Gables Museum at Silver Bush is the most commercialized of the truly historic sites, with a tearoom, antiques shop, and "Matthew's buggy ride," but it is nevertheless, by any standard, still tasteful and sensible. Swing sets sit on an expanse of lawn, the buggy ride is evocative and scenic, and the museum offers some truly meaningful artifacts, especially for older kids. A crazy quilt stitched by Montgomery, for example, is displayed with a quote from her diary talking about how long she labored over it and how much she enjoyed the work. Readers will remember how Anne, unlike her creator, found it impossible to sit and sew.

Nearby, another house associated with Montgomery (that of her paternal grandparents) has been turned into a museum, too. This site will have little appeal for kids, because the guide launches into a sort of script describing Montgomery's prominent relatives and their lives and times.

Close by the national park in Cavendish are two private enterprises geared to families. Avonlea is a reproduction nineteenth-century village with costumed docents and activities, and although an admission fee is charged, it isn't quite a theme park—fast-food stands and tacky souvenir shops are outside, not inside, the village. Across the street, Rainbow Valley is a curiosity having nothing to do with *Anne of Green Gables,* but it has a wacky charm of its own. It's hard to describe—it mixes down-home, teeny-scale elements of Epcot, miniature golf, and an amusement park, yet the setting is one of rolling lawns and shade trees. To those of us "from away," it seems like an incredibly benign and amusing example of commercial development.

Elsewhere on the island, the Confederation Trail is a treasure for families. Stretching from one end of the island to the other on a former railroad bed, the level trail is used by walkers and bikers. It winds through farm country, in and out of villages, and along rivers and beaches. We rented bikes from Trailside Café, Inn, and Adventures, which has an excellent selection for families, including toddler trailers, child seats, and kid-size bikes, and had a great afternoon's ride, picking wild apples, blueberries, and blackberries from the side of the path as we went. There are also seal-watching boat trips from the Murray River area, notable for being on the calm river and therefore easier than many such excursions for young children.

Names and Numbers

Tourism PEI
West Royalty Industrial Park
53 Watt Ave.
Charlottetown, PEI
(888) PEI-PLAY
www.peiplay.com

Confederation Centre for
    the Arts
(*Anne of Green Gables—
    The Musical*)
(800) 565-0278
(902) 566-1267
www.confederationcentre.
    com

Anne's Tea Party
100 Queen St.
Charlottetown, PEI
(902) 894-4141
www.annesteaparty.com
Open June–mid-Oct.

Green Gables PEI National
    Park
Off Rte. 6, west of Rte. 13
Cavendish, PEI
(902) 963-3370
www.parkscanada.gc.ca/
    gables
Open daily May 1–Oct. 31;
call regarding Nov.–Apr.
hours; "chore demonstrations"
in July and Aug.

Anne of Green Gables
Museum at Silver Bush
Rte. 20
Park Corner, PEI
(902) 436-7329
(902) 886-2884
www.annesociety.org/anne
Open May 15–Oct. 31.

Outside Expeditions
    (canoes, etc.)
Bryon and Shirley Wright
North Rustico, PEI
(902) 963-3366
(800) 207-3899
www.getoutside.com

Capt. Garry's Seal and
    Bird-watching Cruises
(800) 496-2494
(902) 962-2494

Trailside Café, Inn, and
    Adventures
109 Main St.
Mount Stewart, PEI
Rte. 22, off Rte. 2 at junction
    of Confederation Trail
(902) 676-3130
(888) 704-6595
www.peisland.com/trailside

A Bear Called Paddington (1958)
& Other Titles

BY **MICHAEL BOND**
Illustrated by **PEGGY FORTNUM**

London, England

"L ondon's such a big place when you've nowhere to go," says Mrs. Brown when she first meets a lost little bear in Paddington Station. Indeed, London is a big city for any small bear . . . or small child. On top of its seven million residents, it has an overlay of twenty-eight million visitors a year! But with Paddington as a guide, the teeming world of train stations, Underground, department stores, big black taxis, and London theater is all distilled to a manageable—and amusing—size. —CDB

This trip is ideal for families with readers between the ages of 8 and 11, but younger and older siblings will enjoy London.

The Books

One day in Paddington Station, the Brown family finds a confused-looking little bear wearing a most unusual wide-brimmed hat and sitting on a battered suitcase. When they ask if he needs help, he reveals that he's just arrived as a stowaway, all the way from Darkest Peru, having been lovingly sent off by his Aunt Lucy, who had to go into a home for retired bears. He has no idea what to do next, and the marmalade jar hanging from a string around his neck is empty. Mrs. Brown immediately worries about the little bear, and when she sees a sign on his suitcase that says, "Please Look After This Bear. Thank You," she decides to take him to the Brown household for a few days, despite Mr. Brown's uncertainty. Because he says his name is "a Peruvian one which no one can understand," he is dubbed Paddington, and he is taken home to meet the Brown children, Judy and Jonathan, and the family housekeeper and cook, the irascible Mrs. Bird. Once he arrives in the Brown household, of course, he's there to stay.

This sets the stage for a series of adventures based around this odd little bear, whose naivete, curiosity, small size, and enthusiasm get him into all sorts of scrapes. "Things are always happening to me," he says in the first few pages. "I'm that sort of bear." Not coincidentally, children are blessed with the same naivete, curiosity, small size, and enthusiasm, which is why reading about his exploits in the teeming metropolis of London makes fine urban-travel preparation for any child.

Your children will giggle and identify when Paddington gets in his first London taxi and gets chided by the driver for being "sticky." And when he doesn't want to part with his ticket for the Underground (he thinks he gets to keep the ticket forever, because the Browns paid good money for it). And when he tries to run up the down escalator in the Underground. And when he gets queasy on the lift (elevator) in Barkridges, the huge department store, then manages to knock down the store's elaborate window display. And when he smuggles his marmalade sandwich into the fancy London theater and then drops it on someone's head. Paddington's exploits, in fact, are often exactly like those of the average energetic 5-year-old child, and even wise, mature 11-year-olds find themselves charmed by the little bear and his well-intentioned mishaps. Maybe they remember being so naive way, way back when they were little kids.

THE PADDINGTON LIBRARY

My 10-year-old daughter Erin had no interest in reading *A Bear Called Paddington*—it seemed dated and boring to her—but after eavesdropping on her little sister's storytime, she got hooked. She appropriated the book for herself, read it, and wanted more. Happily, her school library had several others in the series, and she read them all. Michael Bond kept Paddington in muddles and mishaps for many years, from *Paddington Takes the Air* to *Paddington on Top;* some are still in print, and most can be found at libraries. ⁂ There's a whole other side to Paddington, as well: the simple toddler books, also written by Michael Bond. Instead of narrative chapter book text, these books are often written in simple rhyme. And instead of Peggy Fortnum's breezy sketches, the books are filled with R. W. Alley's boldly colorful illustrations. These are the books most kids know, and they're plentiful in bookstores.

The Experience

Our kids are city kids, but they're California city kids, so London seemed huge, crowded, and full of strange and wonderful things: big black taxis, lurching double-decker buses, cars driving on the wrong side of the road, underground trains, and people filling the sidewalks. Where to begin? We'd just read *Paddington,* and so we let Erin and Emily make the first call: a ride in a London cab. Only problem was, the children weren't yet sticky, having just washed up after breakfast. But the ride was still cause for wonderment, with the huge backseat area, the disorientation of driving on the left, and the bustling city outside our windows.

We passed many a double-decker bus, and the kids grew curiouser and curiouser. Erin knew that in the later books, Paddington becomes very fond of riding on the top deck of a double-decker bus with his friend Mr. Gruber, the antiques dealer from Portobello Road. (Paddington loves Mr. Gruber because he "explains things" to the oft-confused little bear.) "We should ride a bus next, because it was one of Paddington's most favorite things," said Erin; her little sister agreed, always enthusiastic about riding on any form of public transportation. So we exited the taxi at Trafalgar Square to buy tickets for the buses run by the Original London Sight-seeing Tours. Even though it was drizzling, the kids insisted on sitting up top—fortunately, they'd worn their Paddington-like hats and raincoats.

Thus began a memorable hour together. The kids tuned out much of the tour guide's historical talk, as kids are wont to do, though they did like a few of the corny jokes. They focused instead on getting wet, hanging their heads over the railing, looking for pigeons and police officers, and getting sticky by eating gummy bears ("Get it?" Emily said over and over. "*Gummy* bears . . . *Paddington* Bear. Get it?"). From time to time they were wowed, especially by the House of Commons and Buckingham Palace. Eventually, of course, the thrill of riding up top started to pale just a little, and thus began the repeated trips up and down the narrow spiral staircase, just because it was there. Soon our guide was getting annoyed.

"What do you think Paddington would do now?" I asked Emily.

"Well, he would probably have to get off the bus, because he would have got in trouble for getting marmalade in the driver's hair," she said. "Maybe we should get off so we don't get in trouble."

Wise words indeed.

The Itinerary

You don't need to set off on a precise itinerary to follow in Paddington's footsteps through London. Instead, think of *A Bear Called Paddington*'s chapters as snapshots that will prepare kids for a visit to London. And when they find themselves in Paddington-style situations—perhaps accidentally knocking down a department-store display or unintentionally landing in a place they shouldn't be—don't be too hard on them. Mr. and Mrs. Brown understood that little Paddington wasn't yet savvy to the ways of the big city, and little children aren't savvy, either.

The one mandatory place to visit is, of course, Paddington Station, where the Peruvian bear was discovered. It's located in Paddington, a district on the north end of London known for its white-stucco Victorian houses, its vibrant ethnic communities, and, of course, its imposing train station. We happened to need to visit Paddington Station anyway, and if you're making any day trips out of London, or taking the express train to Heathrow, you may also find yourself headed there. Adults will appreciate the grandeur of the 1851 station, with its awe-inspiring iron-girder roof; the kids will appreciate the many trains waiting to depart for seemingly exotic destinations (though no trains for Peru, sadly), not to mention the many venues for snacks. Paddington's first teatime took place in his namesake station, and by all means follow his lead, stopping at one of the snack bars or cafés for something wet and something sticky.

Take note that Paddington Station is just a few blocks north of wonderful Hyde Park; enter the park at the Westbourne Street entrance, veer right around the Long Water pond, and you'll find the famed Peter Pan statue. For a bonus adventure that Paddington would have loved (causing a wet ruckus in the process), rent a paddleboat on the pond.

Otherwise, just keep Paddington in mind as you explore London. Your journeys will most likely include trips on the Underground; by all means let the kids try to go up the down escalator (just make sure they stay out of the way of hurried commuters). Make sure to ride in at least one big black taxi and a few double-decker buses. You might well want to visit the vast, teeming department store called Selfridges (known for its amazing food hall), which was the model for Barkridges, where Paddington causes various problems. In a later book, he gets tangled in a revolving door in another fancy department store called Crumbold and Ferns, inspired by Marks and Spencer—and chances are high that your kids will tangle with a few revolving doors.

Stop for hot cocoa for your "elevenses," the late-morning refreshment break that Paddington likes to take with Mr. Gruber. If you pass a toy store, consider splurging on a small stuffed Paddington, who might make an excellent traveling companion.

As you travel the city, talk with your kids about what it feels like to be a small stranger in a big place. Share stories of how each of you—even the grown-ups—have had Paddington experiences. And figure out what you learned from those experiences. For as the lovable little bear discovers, making mistakes can be a great way to learn.

Names and Numbers

British Tourist Authority
551 Fifth Ave., 7th floor
New York City
(800) 462-2748
www.visitbritain.com

Paddington Station
Eastbourne Terrace and
    Praed St.
London
(44) (8457) 484950 (British
    rail services)

The Original London
    Sight-seeing Tours
Board at Trafalgar Square or
    Green Park tube stop
(44) (020) 88771722

London Tourist Information
    Centres
Victoria Station forecourt,
    Selfridges, Harrods,
    and Heathrow
Open Mon.–Sat. 8 A.M.–
7 P.M. Sun. 8 A.M.–5 P.M.

The Black Stallion (1941)

BY WALTER FARLEY

Belmont Park, Long Island, New York

*E*scapist reading of the purest, most enjoyable kind, this classic tale of a wild black stallion tamed by a teenage New York boy begins on a ship off the coast of India, but the true heart of the story takes place at Belmont Park racetrack. A paddock tour and visit to an early-morning exercise session offers a horse lover's view that's more fun for kids than the actual races. —SLT

This trip is ideal for families with readers between the ages of 8 and 13 and their older siblings.

The Book

Walter Farley was in high school in Brooklyn when he began writing this book, and it was published while he was still an undergraduate at Columbia. A professional horseman uncle provided him with the knowledge that gave his work credibility, but surely his youth allowed him a certain cut-to-the-chase enthusiasm that has given *The Black Stallion* the stuff to grab and hold young readers for some fifty years. This chapter book is most popular with children ages 10 to 13.

The Black Stallion is a lean storytelling machine, as swift as the stallion at its center, as perfect an expression of the heroic formula tale as can be imagined. Its human protagonist,

Alec, is an upstanding youth who is returning from a summer in India visiting his upstanding (and manly) missionary uncle, from whom he learned much about horse handling. The book's animal protagonist, the Black, as he comes to be known, is characterized as wild, free, and misunderstood. The Black is first seen killing a man while being brutally loaded onto the ship Alec is taking home. By the third chapter the boy and the horse are shipwrecked together on an island, Alec having freed the penned stallion as the ship went down and then saved himself by grabbing the swimming animal's halter. By the fifth chapter (nineteen days later), Alec has managed to feed himself and the horse with seaweed as well as tame and ride the horse, so he's ready to be rescued when a ship shows up.

The adult reader can't help but smile at such efficiency of plot, but this book isn't for adults—it speaks directly to the limited but earnest worldview of the young. Need to survive on a desert island? Find the seaweed you learned about in science class. Need to get home from South America with a horse? Wire your parents for money—they'll be waiting patiently for you in New York even though you're the only survivor of a shipwreck and have been believed dead for almost a month. Need to get the horse from the ship to a stable near your home? Here comes a newspaper reporter with a horse trailer, not to mention a retired famous jockey who happened to move in next door to your parents.

But this very efficiency makes *The Black Stallion* gripping. No character is introduced who won't have a pivotal role in the proceedings. No scene is sketched that slows the momentum of the tale.

Alec returns to his home in Flushing, New York, with the black stallion. He goes to school, does his chores, and, with the help of his retired jockey/trainer neighbor, Henry, begins to train the Black to race. The challenges are huge—not only does the horse run so fast and hard that Alec sometimes passes out while he's riding, but the boy must keep the training secret from his parents and keep up his schoolwork at the same time.

It all begins to come together during middle-of-the-night training sessions at Belmont Park. Henry has an old friend who lets them sneak onto the track so the wild horse can learn to run in this formal setting. Word begins to spread, and soon some reporters are brought to the track. After these hard-boiled, laconic, hat-wearing newsmen observe Alec and the Black at Belmont, clocking their speed on stopwatches and then rushing off to meet an early-morning copy deadline, there's no going back. Alec and the Black will race against champions.

The final, exciting race is in Chicago, with Alec's parents on hand to witness his triumph. But a mystery about the black stallion's pedigree lingers, leaving the door open for the sequels *The Black Stallion Returns, The Son of the Black Stallion,* and so on, through another twenty titles.

For reluctant readers, *The Black Stallion* might just be a breakthrough title, with its well-written scenes of the boy's mighty physical efforts, its fast-paced plot, and its satisfying but open-ended outcomes that make you want to continue reading the series.

The Experience

We arrived at Belmont Park at 7:30 in the morning, and the horses were already out in force. Perhaps if you come to Breakfast at Belmont right when it opens at 7, you'll see some of the animals as they first head outside, but many of them come out at first light, which, during the time of year we visited, would have been at 5:30 A.M.

As it was, my friend's son Danny had reluctantly rolled out of bed at 6 that Sunday, but though he was sleepy he knew that Alec had risen at 1:30 A.M. to go to Belmont with the Black three nights a week, so his only real complaints were about the music on the radio stations I had set in the car. As usual.

When we arrived at Belmont Park we felt like we'd entered a new world. How could a place so green, so bucolic, be just minutes from the skyscrapers of Manhattan? But there it was: a 450-acre oasis that, we would soon discover, was indeed a world apart.

Breakfast at Belmont is a low-key affair—no pomp or circumstance, and none of the high-energy ambience you'd expect at a major sports venue. The program consists of breakfast overlooking the track, a lecture/demonstration complete with a live horse, and a tram tour of the paddock area.

The minute we set foot in the so-called café (more akin to a fast-food joint), we were mesmerized by the sight of the thoroughbreds moving around the track. Some ran. Some trotted. Some walked. There was no intensity, no sprinting-down-the-stretch, nose-to-nose excitement, just the arresting sight of absolutely magnificent animals going about their daily business under the tutelage of loving trainers.

We began to better understand some of the descriptions in *The Black Stallion* that seemed a bit baroque when we read them, like when Farley talks about the stallion's "small, savagely beautiful head," or how "his action shifted marvelously as his powerful legs swept over the ground."

As we ate breakfast, a track hostess gave a running talk from her perch along the outside rail. She regaled us with information about the horses, the jockeys, the track itself, and the world of Belmont. We learned why some horses were running hard, some just trotting, some walking, and still others sprinting across the grass. (It all depends on where each is in its training regimen.) We learned that to "hack the horse" means to train on grass, and that to work "in company" is to run two or more horses together to accustom them to race conditions.

While eating, you can watch the horses through huge windows from inside. If you want to see them come up from the paddock area, there's a runway that splits the middle of the stands and a walkway adjacent to the runway. Danny also liked standing by the rail trackside and seeing the horses up close as they trotted and galloped by—you can really hear them breathing when they're running.

Although Danny didn't spot anyone he thought was as young as Alec among the track personnel, the training jocks— known as "red jackets" because that's what they wear look quite young to adult eyes. There were plenty of kids among the breakfast visitors, from 6 months through 10 years. When our guide took us outside to a grassy spot near the end of the grandstand, where a young woman introduced us to a retired thoroughbred (making Danny think of the old horse Napoleon in the book), I noticed the kids' different reactions. A brother-sister team ages 6 and 8 seemed indifferent and continued to play the tag game they'd begun inside. Two slightly older girls, about 7 and 9, were fascinated and clearly loved being able to talk to the horse and pet its nose. Danny had a great time, showing off his knowledge by asking intelligent questions as the guide explained the equipment used to care for the horses and described the equine life: daily workouts, baths, and innumerable brushings. But poor Tommy, a 3-year-old flaming redhead, was absolutely terrified of everything—especially the horse!

We then boarded a tram for a ten-minute narrated tour of the paddock and stable. Back here, behind the scenes, we really got a sense of the world that Alec and the Black were learning about: the insulated, self-sustaining world of the racetrack. In addition to the red jackets, trainers, jockeys, owners, and jockeys' agents we'd seen out by the track, we now saw grooms, stable hands, and security and maintenance workers. Some 2,200 horses are stabled at Belmont Park in racing season, and hundreds of people work there to take care of them.

All pedestrians and vehicles must yield the right-of-way to any horse anywhere on the grounds, so several times while we were on the tram tour, we had to stop and let horses pass. This seemed like a good power shift to Danny and the horse-loving girls, and they were fascinated, too, by hearing that the oval-shaped barns contain indoor walking tracks on which the horses are cooled down after a hard workout or exercised on bad-weather days.

The best part of the tour was last: a starting-gate demonstration. Even the kids who'd never seen a horse race had seen a cartoon of one, so all knew what the gate was for and, when invited to do so, happily rushed into one of the numbered places and pretended to be thoroughbreds at the Belmont Stakes. While the adults (who'd also gamely assumed places as horses) listened to an explanation of the gate's complex electromagnetic mechanics, the kids neighed, whinnied, and pawed the ground. When the guide took the announcer's part and, over clangs and buzzers, shouted, "And they're off!" we all rushed out. Laughing, the grown-ups stopped after a few paces, but the kids kept running and running and running. Like the black stallion when he ran, they were "once again wild and free."

The Itinerary

Although children in racetrack-savvy families attend meets all the time, we don't think your average kid gets nearly as much from an afternoon at the races as he or she does from a morning at a workout session. It can be very exciting if you're on the rail when the horses run by, but the action lasts for only about a minute at a time, with great pauses for betting and setting up the next race. Adults fill the time with frantic efforts to figure out which horse to bet on, but kids, in our experience, get bored and start wandering around looking for mischief.

So don't worry about sticking around for the races, which begin more than three hours after the tour ends. Just make Breakfast at Belmont an early-morning excursion and leave it at that.

Don't be fooled into imagining that this is a gourmet breakfast shared with the high-society set. The ambience is utilitarian at best. Aside from the vast windows that look out on the track, the décor of the restaurant is strictly plastic. The tables barely hold four people, and each comes with a mini-TV on which fans watch the races later in the day. The menu consists of scrambled eggs or pancakes with perhaps some bacon or a bagel—it's mediocre food (albeit cheap), but it doesn't much matter. You're here for the horses.

And the setting is wonderful, with the lush green infield, the dark brown track, the infield pond, and the lavish and luxuriant vegetation all around. And, oh yes, all those horses.

Names and Numbers

Belmont Park
Exit 26-D, Cross Island
    Parkway
2150 Hempstead Turnpike
Elmont, New York
(516) 488-6000
www.nyracing.com/belmont
Breakfast at Belmont is offered during racing season (May–Jul. and Sept.–Oct.; check for dates) and on weekends and holidays 7–9:30 A.M.; narration and guided tours begin at about 8:30. Admission free.

Brighty of the Grand Canyon (1953)

BY MARGUERITE HENRY

Grand Canyon National Park, Arizona

Whether it's for a single afternoon as part of a family road trip or for a week-long stay that fulfills a dream of hiking or rafting, the Grand Canyon is one of America's most frequently visited national parks. *Brighty of the Grand Canyon* is a book that's fun to read before or during a trip to this iconic American landscape. The little wild burro's adventures give kids reference points in all that scenic grandeur.   —SLT

This trip is ideal for families with readers between the ages of 8 and 12.

The Book

In the 1920s, when the Grand Canyon had just become a national park, magazine stories about the exploits of a wild burro there began to appear. These stories celebrated the colorful personality of a critter whose antics captured the imagination of park visitors. Bright Angel was the burro's name, and his history was well known. Like the other wild burros then found in the canyon, he'd come with prospectors. The date of his arrival, 1892, was known because he'd been found by locals at a campsite that was mysteriously abandoned by the men who'd made it. He was famous throughout the little communities of the area because of his amusing ability to, as one chronicler put it, "maintain his liberty for thirty years."

Brighty, it seems, was a bit of a freeloader, and he didn't quite commit to the pack-animal role. He'd hang around settlements and campgrounds, accept food, and even agree to be mounted or have a pack placed upon him. But never for long. He'd slip away from his tether in the night, or leave the line during a trek and hide in the bushes until the expedition was delayed and the humans exasperated. The usual techniques, including putting a bell on the burro's bridle, didn't discourage him. He learned to walk so quietly that he could sneak away even when belled. Over and over he'd submit to capture, enjoy a few good meals, and then gnaw through his tether in the night and sneak away.

The tragic disappearance of Brighty's original owners was a not-uncommon occurrence in the wild and dangerous Grand Canyon of the late nineteenth century, and Marguerite Henry's fictionalization gives a credible historic underpinning to a child's adventure tale. Her use of actual Grand Canyon settings is also true to life and provides an accurate introduction to the area's geography.

For children between 8 and 10, *Brighty of the Grand Canyon* is pretty exciting, with a plot that includes a murder, a teenage boy's near-starvation in a snowbound cabin, and a fight (almost to the death) between a mature Brighty and another male for dominance of a wild burro herd. For kids between 10 and 12, *Brighty of the Grand Canyon* opens a window on national park history, with an appearance by President Teddy Roosevelt and a scene of the opening of the suspension footbridge across the Colorado River. For all readers, it's a satisfying and imaginative expansion of the true story. Marguerite

Henry's gift is to be able to provide an unsentimental glimpse into the mind of this wild burro.

The fun of reading the book before your trip is that when you arrive at the edge of the Grand Canyon and are numbed into awe, the bits of Brighty's story floating in your head will allow you to spot little details of the scenery and give them significance. This is especially useful with children, who sometimes cannot grasp a picture as big as the scene before them at the rim of the canyon.

The fun of reading about Brighty while you're staying in Grand Canyon Village is that it allows your explorations and your relaxing time to be all centered on the park. It's nicer in so many ways for kids to sit back at the motel or campground and read another chapter of this book than to turn away from the timelessness of the canyon with TV or video games.

HORSES, HORSES EVERYWHERE

Traveling families with 9- to 12-year-olds (especially those with horse lovers) would do well to keep an eye on the more than a dozen Marguerite Henry books that are fictionalized accounts of place-specific American horse history. *Misty of Chincoteague,* her Newbery Honor Book about the wild ponies on the islands off Virginia and Maryland, is well known, but there are other titles to look for. *Mustang, Spirit of the West* is about the woman who saved the wild horses of Nevada; *Black Gold* and *Born to Trot* accurately depict the world of racehorses in Kentucky; *San Domingo, the Medicine Hat Stallion* takes place in pre-Civil War Wyoming; and *Justin Morgan Had a Horse* traces the history of the Morgan breed from its origins in Vermont.

The Experience

Even the forest ranger I spoke to said he had trouble getting perspective as he looked out at the Grand Canyon, and he'd been hiking its trails for a year as part of the safety patrol. For children standing at the edge and gazing out over the stone walls at the South Rim, this great American spectacle can quickly blur into unreality.

But as my husband and I and our daughter Patricia stood with another family at the rim, 9-year-old Ryan, our friend's son, was fully engaged, and asked the ranger to help us decode the view. First, the ranger pointed out Bright Angel Trail, one of the most asked-about features of the landscape because it stands out, even from a great distance: a light-colored line crossing a dark, flat area halfway down the immense canyon.

"That's the one that Brighty made, following the creek!" said Ryan.

It amazed and gratified him to see the evidence of Brighty's existence with his own eyes. Next, the ranger helped him see the place on the far side of the canyon where the creek cuts in and Bright Angel Trail continues up the canyon wall to the North Rim.

As Ryan continued to pepper the ranger with questions about locations from the book, the rest of us took pictures or just gazed, focusing first on one amazing formation or detail of color, then another. Those of us, adult or child, who had read *Brighty of the Grand Canyon* were pleased with our more intimate sense of knowing the landscape. We could imagine the charming figure of Brighty the burro trotting down Bright Angel Trail, galloping around the Tonto Plateau (a dominant feature of the view from the village) with his herd of mares and foals, and finally emerging at the top of the North Rim, an impossible distance away.

Many of Brighty's adventures took place at the North Rim,

and there's a statue of him at the new visitors center there. But most visitors to the Grand Canyon come, as our family did, only to the South Rim. As we discovered, a satisfying experience on the trail of Brighty can be had even by kids who are at the canyon for only a few hours.

Among the campfire presentations, guided walks and ranger talks we joined were several that made reference to landmarks and other aspects of the Brighty story. Adults who read Marguerite Henry's acknowledgments will find the names of important people in Grand Canyon history (cougar hunters, ranchers, artists, and prospectors) who were still alive when she did her research and who figure in the talks and brochures.

And we found that you don't actually have to walk or ride on Bright Angel Trail to get some of the flavor of the experience. Although our group wasn't signed up for the mule ride, we'd been told that watching the gruff wranglers (several of whom are legendary for their irascible personalities) prepare the dudes for the excursion was a show in itself. Amusingly, it was true. Along with a few other "audience members," Ryan and I laughed as a cowboy as grizzled as those in the book told the riders to keep their mounts close together on the trail ("These mules are going into the canyon because you want to go, not because they want to go. They've been there.") and advised them not to lean away from the edge as they rode ("We know that's hard with nothing but 600 feet of air between you and the ground, but these saddles are not nailed on.").

The burros are gone from the Grand Canyon, but Brighty's spirit roams "forever wild, forever free," and that's as true today as it was when Henry published her book. Although some might wish for a book that extols the free spirit of a native species rather than an introduced one, this particular half-wild burro is an enduring symbol of the complexities of even defining concepts like "wild" and "free."

The Itinerary

Accept no substitutions. Stay at the Bright Angel Lodge at Grand Canyon Village. Like the older and grander El Tovar, Bright Angel Lodge, dating from 1935, is part of the historic section of the village and is situated so you're always glimpsing the canyon, even if you're just taking the kids for an ice cream cone. The main lodge is a dramatic log-and-stone building, and the aura of Brighty's pioneering era is very much present. Rooms vary—why not try for one of the fireplace-warmed log cabins right at the edge of the rim?

You'll also be only steps away from the Bright Angel Trail trailhead. Mule rides depart daily in season, so after enjoying a sunrise view of the canyon, head for the 7:15 predeparture gathering for a glimpse of Brighty-like animals up close.

For ambitious families who plan to take the famous mule ride down Bright Angel Trail (and you know who you are and that you'll need reservations way in advance), reading *Brighty of the Grand Canyon* will inform and enhance the experience. True, Brighty's a wild burro, not a trained mule, and the burros have been removed from the canyon because of the environmental damage they caused. But mules and burros are species that share both surefootedness and stubbornness. Brighty, in spite of his tricks, had a patience in letting children ride him that was as legendary as the patience and endurance of today's Grand Canyon mule train.

There are height and weight requirements for participation in these popular one- and two-day trail rides, but many children 10 and older are up to the demands, which include exerting authority over your mount and being able to pee behind a rock should the need arise.

Later, board the shuttle to the West Rim, hopping on and off to walk and gawk. Near the Powell Memorial, you can see the entrance to an old mine, the visible reminder of the prospecting that figures so prominently in the area's history and the book's plot. Check out the various museums, visitor centers, and galleries for exhibits about the human and animal inhabitants of the canyon.

For the very young, the gift shops stock stuffed animals that are cuddlier than the wildlife. Plush squirrels and deer are joined by little mules that can stand in for the burro. *Brighty of the Grand Canyon* is on sale at all the village gift shops as well as at the visitor centers.

If you have only a few hours in the park, be sure to stop at the Yavapi Observation Center, a half mile east of the main visitor center. From its huge windows you'll see—way, way down there—the suspension bridge first trod upon by President Theodore Roosevelt and Bright Angel, known as Brighty, the burro.

Names and Numbers

Grand Canyon National Park
(928) 638-7888 (headquarters
   and information)
www.nps.gov
*Upon arrival, ask at the visitor
center about the many family
programs offered, including
junior ranger programs,
ranger hikes, kids' walks, and
stargazing programs.*

AMFAC Parks and Resorts
(303) 297-2757 (lodge
   reservations, mule trips,
   and tours)
www.grandcanyonlodges.com
A helpful Web site:
   grandcanyon.
   national-park.com

Child of the Owl (1977)

BY LAURENCE YEP

San Francisco, California

*I*n 1964, a streetwise Chinese-American girl is sent to live with her immigrant grandmother, Paw-Paw, and this unlikely (but likable) duo becomes our guide to San Francisco's Chinatown. They lead readers to the same sights we can see today: back-alley herb shops, elderly Chinese men playing chess in the park, roast ducks hanging in windows, and dim sum restaurants selling Paw-Paw's beloved *bao* buns. —CDB

This trip is ideal for families with readers between the ages of 10 and 13.

The Book

To 12-year-old Casey, home has always been wherever her father is. Because he's a less-than-successful gambler by trade, willing to work actual jobs only when money runs out, Barney moves around a lot, always with Casey in tow. They do stints in Fresno and Stockton, Santa Barbara and San Mateo. Casey understands the worlds of bookies and smoky bars, she's found a way to survive regular school changes, and she's used to taking care of herself, because her mother died when she was a baby. Barney is no Ward Cleaver, but he and Casey love each other.

Then Barney gets severely beaten up because of gambling debts, and Casey is forced to go live with her uncle's family in San Francisco. This tough, self-reliant girl is a poor fit with her spoiled, prissy, rich-girl cousins, and soon she's shipped off again to live in Chinatown with her maternal grandmother, Paw-Paw, a Chinese immigrant who does piecework in a sewing shop to make her meager living. Then things get interesting.

Casey and Paw-Paw take a shine to each other, even though they have to share one cockroach-infested tenement room, with a toilet down the hall. But once-tough Casey feels lost and helpless outside those four shabby walls. After her first horrible day at Chinatown's Catholic school, where she is belittled for her ragged hand-me-down uniform, she says:

> *My skin color and different-shaped eyes were like theirs.*
> *Only I didn't want to be like them because they made*
> *me feel rotten and fat and ugly. No one had ever made*
> *me feel like this when I was in the American schools*
> *outside of Chinatown.*

Chinese school is even worse—all the other kids are already well versed in speaking and writing Chinese, but she doesn't have a clue, and the teacher showers her with hostility for being "'Merican-born." She'd always been somewhat of a loner, but she'd never felt lonely like this before.

Author Laurence Yep grew up in Chinatown, which is why this sixth- to eighth-grade chapter book and its characters are so rich and true. And no character is richer than tiny, gray-haired Paw-Paw, who becomes the real star of the story. As she flips playing cards, listens to American pop radio, and takes Casey to Chinese movies and shops, she helps her granddaughter discover herself. From Paw-Paw, Casey learns about her mother. She learns about Chinese culture, religion, and food, and even masters chopsticks. She learns about what life was like in China, and how hard it is for the immigrant to adapt to America, which changes her resentment and anger toward Chinatown's difficult old people to understanding. And Paw-Paw tells her that feeling alone is in her blood, because everyone in their family is a child of the Owl Spirit, which according to Chinese legend means they are strong-willed, fiercely independent, and even a little evil.

As the book progresses, Casey's spirit is tested, and her father breaks her heart. Ultimately, she makes her stand—and her peace—in Chinatown, with Paw-Paw. She sees that while she has some of the fierce, independent spirit of a Chinese owl, she has learned to temper it with the wise, calm spirit of an American owl.

The Experience

It was lunchtime, and we were en route to have dim sum. Reading *Child of the Owl* had left Erin and me hungry. The scene describing Casey's trek from food shop to food shop, determined to spend an unexpected gift of $5 on a feast for Paw-Paw, had us dreaming of *bao* buns and dumplings. (Erin's a notoriously picky eater, but she's crazy for potstickers.) So we walked to Chinatown from our Financial District hotel, entering the ceremonial gateway at Grant Avenue and Bush Street. Our destination was a restaurant called Lichee Garden, where, friends had promised, the dim sum was fresh and delicious.

There was only one problem, according to Erin and her 11-year-old legs—Lichee Garden was way over at the other end of Chinatown. What at first seemed like a problem, however, became a blessing. For during our twelve-block stroll, we zigzagged through the whole of Chinatown, absorbing daily life in one of the nation's most intriguing and lively neighborhoods. It was a weekday, which meant that Grant Avenue and Stockton

Street weren't as crowded with tourists as usual, though it was hardly deserted—the sidewalks of Chinatown's commercial blocks are always thick with people.

On our walk, we passed lots of old women who reminded us of Paw-Paw and lots of old men who reminded us of her friend Mr. Jeh. Many of them were carrying small bags of food or were in the process of buying food. We passed stores filled with postcards and souvenirs (many of which were not even Chinese, as the book notes) and, after we jogged over to Stockton Street, stores filled with food. We passed tiny shops selling tea, shops selling herbs, shops selling Chinese-language newspapers and books, and laundromats . . . a lot of laundromats.

We stopped at an elementary school, where a crowd of children filled a cramped concrete yard, yelling and running and jumping rope. Erin loves watching other kids, especially if they're in school and she's not.

"This looks just like Casey's school!" she said, and I replied that it might have been (densely packed Chinatown has several schools).

"But I don't hear any of them talking Chinese," she said.

I explained that many of the kids were probably second- or third-generation Asian-Americans who may not even hear Chinese at home—and some of them weren't Chinese at all, but Vietnamese, Korean, and Cambodian, from a newer wave of immigration. This led to a good conversation about what it would be like to move thousands of miles away from home, to a place full of strange and sometimes frightening new things.

By the time we reached Lichee Garden, we were famished and ready to sit down. We shared an order of fluffy white *bao* buns filled with sweet pork, in honor of Casey, who loved them. We had an order of Erin's favorite, meaty potstickers, and a plate of another of Casey's favorites, chicken chow mein. Alas, there was no roast duck on the lunch menu—but as Casey learns from Paw-Paw, it's a dinner dish, anyway. So we made a plan to stop later at the best-looking Stockton Street shop for a roast duck to take back for a hotel-room dinner that night, to eat while we watched a martial-arts movie on the VCR.

The Itinerary

Chinatown is high on the list for any visitor to San Francisco, and the experience for older kids (10 and up) will be made more resonant by reading *Child of the Owl* first. Yep set his story in 1964, so he could describe the smaller, poorer Chinatown of his youth, before a more relaxed immigration law was passed (which led to huge growth in Chinatown) and before more stringent rules on housing and workplace standards. But the essence of Chinatown remains the same, as do many of the sights and sounds that Casey experiences.

Basically, a *Child of the Owl* itinerary involves exploring the neighborhood on foot. If you visit by day, make sure to stop at Portsmouth Square, the only open green space in Chinatown and a place that was important to Paw-Paw. Back then, it was just a shabby piece of lawn where Chinese men played a form of chess and women talked. Today's park is more developed, with playground equipment and benches, but it's still pretty modest and cramped compared to most city parks. And it remains much used by locals, who range from old men playing chess to kids on scooters and skateboards.

Even back in 1964, Grant Avenue had schlocky souvenir shops whose merchandise could just as well have been sold at Fisherman's Wharf, and that's true now more than ever. But Grant is still worth a stroll if you're seeking a souvenir—in between the schlock are such worthy places as the Chinatown Kite Shop (an incredible collection of kites), Chew Chong Tai and Co. (the oldest store in Chinatown, selling supplies for calligraphy and art), and several shops offering child-size embroidered pajamas and slippers. Most stores are open late into the evening, so if you're exploring after dinner (the better to experience the neon glow and evening bustle), you'll still be able to browse.

As you walk through Chinatown, make sure to take little detours down the small alleys and side streets. That's where you'll see the Chinatown that Paw-Paw lived in: tightly packed apartment buildings (with laundry fluttering from windows, just as in Casey's day), tiny herb shops, Chinese benevolent societies, temples, and small garment factories like the one in which Paw-Paw worked. On Ross Alley, between Grant and Stockton, stop at Golden Gate Fortune Cookies and watch through the window as the bakers make cookies. You'll probably pass at least one elementary school; with luck, you'll get to see the schoolkids in action, as we did.

The video revolution brought with it the demise of the theaters that showed Hong Kong martial-arts movies, so you won't be able to go to a movie the way Paw-Paw and Casey did. But little video stores abound in Chinatown, so stop in one to pick out a movie to watch at your hotel. Casey drew inspiration from seeing women kick-boxers back in the '60s; you and your child can get the same inspiration from renting *Crouching Tiger, Hidden Dragon* (or maybe an older Michelle Yeoh movie). Pick a video store full of Chinese-language signs and posters and let your child negotiate the rental on her own, to better understand how Casey could feel like a foreigner in her own country.

Finally, of course, you have to eat. Chinatown's food makes a big impression on Casey, and because of their poverty, she and Paw-Paw treasure a rare meal out, even if it's just chow mein. As you explore Stockton Street and Grant Avenue, Chinatown's two commercial streets, you'll see burnished roast ducks hanging in windows, mountains of Chinese greens, strings of Chinese sausage, and tanks filled with live seafood—and you'll soon be ravenous.

If it's breakfast or lunchtime, you won't do better for dumplings and chow mein than Lichee Garden, a quiet restaurant on the north of Chinatown, where it merges into North Beach. Or to experience a typical teeming dim sum emporium, try New Asia, a thousand-seat restaurant jammed with noisy people and women pushing stainless-steel carts laden with dumplings. If you're going out to dinner, share Casey and Paw-Paw's joy at the unspeakable luxury of duck by ordering a Peking duck feast at Yuet Lee, a funky dive with terrific food (including great seafood); Lichee Garden also has good duck.

Names and Numbers

San Francisco Visitors and
    Convention Bureau
201 3rd St., Ste. 900
San Francisco
(415) 391-2000
www.sfvisitor.org

Lichee Garden
1416 Powell St.
San Francisco
(415) 397-2290
Open daily for breakfast,
lunch, and dinner.

New Asia
772 Pacific Ave.
San Francisco
(415) 391-6666
Open daily for breakfast,
lunch, and dinner.

Yuet Lee
1300 Stockton St.
San Francisco
(415) 982-6020
Open daily except Tues. for
lunch and dinner (until
3 A.M.).

Eloise (1955)

by **Kay Thompson**
Illustrated by **Hilary Knight**

New York City

*F*or some kids, New York means the Statue of Liberty and the Empire State Building. For others, it means only one thing:  the Plaza Hotel. If Eloise could pass day after fabulous day within the gilded walls of this famed hotel, then any fan of hers should plan on spending at least an afternoon here. Or moving in for a *rawther* long time. —CDB

This trip is ideal for families with readers between the ages of 6 and 10, but kids from 4 to 13 will enjoy it.

The Book

Eloise was a roaring success from the day it was published in 1955—the very day, because, as Kay Thompson's biographer Marie Brenner recounts, on the Friday the printed book hit the Simon and Schuster office, so many staffers went crazy for it that the editor had to order a second printing by noon. The feisty, devilish 6-year-old girl immediately became as real a New Yorker as the Statue of Liberty, and she's been captivating readers—especially young girls—for nearly half a century since.

Part of *Eloise's* success had to do with the era in which it was published. It was the height of the '50s, the days of *Ozzie and Harriet*, well-starched aprons, and women who knew their place in the world. Along came Eloise, a poor little rich girl who lived in the Plaza, did as she pleased, and was *rawther* unusual. Not for her the life of routine domestic humdrum. Who needs cocking and cleaning when you can say, "Charge it, please," whenever you like?

Today, women aren't quite so slotted into roles, and little girls feel freer to be who they want to be. But *Eloise* is every bit as appealing to today's children as it is to nostalgic boomer moms. For today's kids, her physical freedom is envied. Our children are watched and chauffeured, never free to roam and explore by themselves. Eloise, however, wandered for hours through the huge hotel, skating down hallways, crashing weddings, pestering the concierge, writing her name on the wall, hanging out in Catering . . . doing exactly as she pleased, with no interference from Nanny or the never-seen, rarely mentioned mother. Few 6-year-olds today would be allowed to hang out alone in the teeming lobby of an urban hotel. But Eloise did, and she did it with flair.

The flamboyant, childless, Plaza-dwelling Kay Thompson used to insist that she was the last person on earth who would have written a children's book. And yet she perfectly captured the outright joy of being a young child. We adults wonder about the missing mother and the nonexistent father and think how sad a child like that would have really been. But when kids read the book—or you read it to them—they don't bog down in such concerns. They completely identify with a child who would order a room-service raisin for her turtle Skipperdee, wear toe shoes on her ears to lunch, pretend to be a mother with forty children, give her mother's lawyer rubber candy, and pour water down the mail chute. Who cares if your mother's off in Gstaad with an ad man?

The Experience

We felt we had no choice: To have a true Eloise experience, we had to stay at the Plaza. After all, 7-year-old Emily adored her compatriot in exuberant girlhood, and the two of us had to stay *somewhere* in New York. So what if my credit card screamed as it was swiped through at the end of our stay?

If it weren't for Eloise, there wouldn't be any particular reason to choose the Plaza over other big-bucks New York luxury hotels. Its amenities aren't better than anyone else's, its bathrooms are *rawther* dated, and the lobby has no place to sit. But it is a truly grand place, stuffed full of the sort of details that kids associate with glamour: marble, gilt, rococo ornamentation, columns, and enough crystal chandeliers to fill the *Titanic*. Emily's eyes were wide when we checked in, and they stayed wide for the first day; after that, of course, living amid such glamour seemed natural.

After checking in (we had a quiet, comfortable room with *two* chandeliers), we made a beeline for F.A.O. Schwarz across the street, to check out the Eloise section. Emily was dazzled by the stuffed Weenies and Skipperdees, the Eloise books and hat boxes, and the "Do Not Disturb" sign to hang on your bedroom door. The contents of her wallet limited her purchases to two items: a floppy Eloise doll and a pair of pink, rhinestone-studded movie-star sunglasses, which she wore for our entire stay, despite the fact that it was overcast and never got above 20 degrees.

Over the next two days, we modeled ourselves after Eloise and Nanny. We ordered room-service breakfast, just like they did every morning. Emily giggled and said, "Charge it, please," to the waiter, while I swooned at the $65 bill. (Nanny didn't have to care about such things, but I couldn't help myself.) Emily rode the elevator up and down, up and down, for no good reason. She swooped through the lobby in her movie-star sunglasses and fabulous 1950s hand-me-down red wool coat (with black velvet collar), clutching her Eloise doll and attracting smiles and conversation from the doorman, the concierge, the bellman, and many guests.

The first night we scampered to the Terrace Room, where Eloise watched debutantes dance and we watched elegant New Yorkers make speeches for a political fund-raiser. The next night there was what Eloise would have called an "enormous affair" in the Grand Ballroom, so we sneaked in to marvel at the women in gowns and elbow-length gloves and the men in black tie and patent-leather shoes, noshing and dancing and drinking martinis. We visited Hilary Knight's oil painting of Eloise many times, and visited the neighboring fancy chocolate shop just as often. And, of course, we had tea at the Palm Court, where a man who looked exactly like Thomas, Eloise's favorite waiter, poured hot chocolate from a silver pitcher. This inspired Emily to re-create the scene from the book in which Eloise tortures her prissy French tutor, Philip, by repeating everything he says. I said, "How's your hot chocolate, Emily?" And she said, "How's your hot chocolate, Emily?" And so on and so on and so on. She found it absolutely hilarious, and I only pretended to be as annoyed as Philip.

Because we don't actually live at the Plaza, and because I don't have anywhere near the fiscal resources that Eloise's mysterious mother had, Emily couldn't mimic her heroine in the sorts of activities that would result in being presented with either a lawsuit or a hefty repair bill: writing her name

on the walls in red crayon, skiddering a stick along the hall-
way walls, sklonking a staff member in the kneecap, or, most
tempting of all, pouring a pitcher of water down the mail
chute. Although we did spend a long time looking at the mail
chute next to our room, contemplating it. Boy, it would have
been fun. . . .

The Itinerary

You don't need to stay at the Plaza to have a fun Eloise experience. You just need to hang around the place long enough to
get a taste of what life was like for the 6-year-old who called
this hotel home. If you aren't staying, build your visit around
either lunch or tea at the Palm Court; if possible, plan your
visit for a weekday, because both the Palm Court (which
doesn't take tea reservations) and the common rooms are
teeming with day-trip tourists on weekends.

Since Eloise absolutely loves presents, start your adventure
with a shopping trip at F.A.O. Schwarz across the street. The
Eloise section is on the second floor, and it's full of fun stuff. If
you're feeling flush, splurge on one of the hatboxes filled with
toys and Eloise accessories; if you're on a budget, a pair of the
aforementioned movie-star sunglasses will add a lot to a child's
day of pretending to be a rich resident of the Plaza.

Then on to the hotel. Before your meal, allow an hour or
so to explore. Look for Knight's painting of Eloise on the
ground floor. Ride the elevators awhile. Skibble around various
hallways, rooms, and doorways, taking particular care when
opening every exit door to see what interesting things you
might discover. Wander into the Oak Room and see if you can
snatch a "broken mint." If you're staying at the hotel, ask the
concierge if you and your child can go down to Catering,

where Eloise loved to hang out and watch party food get prepared. See if they are setting up for an enormous affair in the Grand Ballroom or a more intimate affair in the Terrace Room.

Eloise lunched regularly at the Palm Court, where she chatted with Thomas the waiter and he slipped her some *gugelhopfen*. You, too, can lunch at the Palm Court and be cared for by a waiter much like Thomas; even more popular is the afternoon tea, when children are poured hot chocolate from silver pitchers. It's fun for a kid to imagine getting hot chocolate like that every day. When the bill comes, give your child the credit card and let her hand it to the waiter, giving her the great fun of saying, "Charge it, please!"

Whether you're staying at the Plaza or somewhere else, try to schedule some wandering time in the evening. There's almost always something going on in at least one of the party rooms; on a good night, you might get several events. Skibble around and see what's going on, and mingle a little with the partygoers. Emily got a thrill just being in the midst of all those fur-coated ladies and tuxedoed men. She envied Eloise, who mingled with them every night.

During a brief foray outside, we hopped into a horse-drawn carriage outside the front door for a ride through Central Park, because it seemed like the sort of thing Eloise's mother's attorney might have sprung for. As for other amusements outside of the Plaza's gilt walls . . . well, Eloise never seemed to leave, so why should we?

STUART LITTLE'S NEW YORK CITY

E. B. White's *Stuart Little* is right up there with *Eloise* in the pantheon of classic children's books set in New York, although the settings aren't nearly as specific as in *Eloise*—Stuart, the two-inch mouse, spends a lot of time either inside the Little family's apartment or, later in the

book, in an unnamed part of upstate New York. But perhaps the book's most memorable scene—when Stuart
becomes a sailor—takes place on the boat pond in Central Park. Before a New York trip, we highly recommend
reading this wonderful book (with its strange, existential
ending) and spending an hour sailing a rented or home-
made boat (empty one-liter water bottles make fine vessels) on the pond. Make sure to allow a little detour time
for the adjacent Alice in Wonderland sculpture, a satisfying piece to climb on and explore.

Names and Numbers

The Plaza Hotel
Fifth Ave. and Central Park
   South
New York City
(212) 759-3000

F.A.O. Schwarz
767 Fifth Ave.
New York City
(212) 644-9400

From the Mixed-up Files of
Mrs. Basil E. Frankweiler (1967)

BY E. L. KONIGSBURG

The Metropolitan Museum of Art, New York City

New York is one of the world's great cultural centers, and the repository of much of that culture is the vast and legendary Metropolitan Museum. Because it is where the Kincaid children live (after running away from home), the Met is the focal point of a *Mixed-up Files* trip. And because the adventures of Claudia and Jamie Kincaid are so enthralling, kids will be happy to immerse themselves in all that great art and culture, just to have a Claudia and Jamie experience.   —CDB

This trip is ideal for families with readers between the ages of 9 and 12, but it works for kids as young as 6 if the book is read to them.

The Book

This Newbery winner may have been published more than thirty years ago, but it's every bit as captivating to today's kids as it was to their parents. Many a third-grade teacher reads it aloud, and millions of kids read it on their own in the fourth, fifth, or sixth grade, either as a class assignment or just for fun.

Its timelessness is due to E. L. Konigsburg's clever story, believable characters, smooth narrative, and sense of humor.

Twelve-year-old Claudia Kincaid is a good girl. She gets perfect grades, is responsible and polite, and does her chores. Her parents seem nice enough, and her brothers aren't too obnoxious. So why does she want to run away? For starters, her parents don't appreciate her enough. (This is a universal kid belief.) Then there's the terrible injustice in being the oldest, not to mention being the only girl, not to mention having to do more chores—having to empty the dishwasher *and* set the table in one night is just too much to ask. (What 12-year-old doesn't have a life full of such injustice?) And finally, there's the monotony of her calm Connecticut life. She craves excitement, beauty, and culture. So Claudia decides to run away to New York, specifically to the Metropolitan Museum of Art, the epitome of beauty and culture for this young suburban snob.

Because her attempts to save money for the adventure have failed, and her brother Jamie is the family tightwad, she convinces him to join her on the adventure. They plan carefully, pack essentials in their book bags and music cases, pretend to set off for school one morning, and instead take the commuter train to Grand Central Station—squabbling all the way. They are opposites, as siblings typically are. Claudia is fastidious, rules-conscious, rather prissy, and careless about money. Jamie is sloppy and more free-spirited, but a savvy money manager. But as they squabble their way to the museum, encountering challenges every step of the way, the narrator, Mrs. Basil E. Frankweiler (a rich old lady who writes the story as a letter to her attorney, Saxonberg), tells us that something important has happened: They have become a team. Sure, they still argue, but each no longer fears that the other will leave. They've learned, deep down, what family really means.

The siblings then take up residence at the Met. Evading guards and other potentially nosy adults, they build a secret life: sleeping in a sixteenth-century canopied bed in the French and English furniture section; bathing at night in one of the fountains (in which they also find a good stash of lunch-money coins); coping with homesickness; and eating in the cafeteria or at the Automat out in the big world. (Because admission at the Met was free in those days—it still is, for kids—they could walk in and out freely during regular hours.)

On their first day in their new home, Jamie and Claudia join a long line of people, curious what the fuss could be about. They file past the museum's newest acquisition, a small statue of an angel, which was bought for a pittance and whose creator is not known for sure, though it is clearly from the Italian Renaissance. Claudia becomes obsessed with solving the mystery of who sculpted the statue—could it be Michelangelo?—and Jamie reluctantly joins in the quest for clues. As their week in the Metropolitan unfolds, they get closer to the answer—and come close to being caught—and Mrs. Frankweiler's story builds to several surprises at the end.

Teachers and parents like this book because it teaches kids about the Italian Renaissance, Michelangelo, and the Metropolitan Museum. But kids love it because it's a fun read, with wonderful characters, a captivating mystery, a solid adventure, and honest laughs.

The Experience

Some kids seem to have an allergic reaction to art museums, and 8-year-old Emily is one of them. She had never lasted more than ten minutes in a museum without collapsing into tears. So despite having just read (and loved) *From the Mixed-up Files of*

Mrs. Basil E. Frankweiler, she was deeply skeptical about a day at the Metropolitan. But we were on vacation in New York, and, like it or not, we were going to the Met. (It is, after all, the single biggest attraction in New York, drawing five and a half million visitors a year.)

One hour later, as we were poring over miniature tomb figures in the Egyptian Wing, it hit me: Not only was Emily not in tears, but she was completely absorbed. How could this be?

Some of the credit was due, of course, to the happy evenings we had spent reading *From the Mixed-up Files of Mrs. Basil E. Frankweiler.* Konigsburg does not wax on about the glories of the museum, knowing full well that it would put the typical fifth-grade reader to sleep. And she readily acknowledges that museum visits can be torture for kids, especially visits of the generic-field-trip variety. To quote Mrs. Frankweiler, who is describing what one field-trip group was doing when its guide asked if there were any questions:

> *At least twelve members of Gr. 6, W.P.S. were busy poking each other. Twelve were wondering when they would eat; four were worried about how long it would be before they could get a drink of water.*

Emily appreciated this honesty, and part of her must have figured that if Konigsburg admitted that kids often find museums boring, but Claudia and Jamie decided the Met was cool anyway, then maybe she'd go in with an open mind.

The rest of the credit for Emily's absorption was due to the Met itself. It was easy to bypass the rooms that I knew would bomb (basically, any room full of paintings), because there was so much more to explore—especially the areas that attracted Claudia and Jamie. Emily wasn't quite as taken with Arms and Armor as Jamie was, being a child more interested in glitter nail polish than weapons. She did think the medieval section was interesting, especially the chapel in which the Kincaids said a prayer. But what really sucked her in was the Egyptian Wing.

"Whoaaaaa," she said when we first walked into the vast skylit chamber that holds the Temple of Dendur. The scale of the room, and the way the sand-colored temple looked imposing and mystical and yet somehow like a really great playhouse, got her attention. Slowly we circled the temple, and on its far side we were surprised to see a fourth-grade class on a field trip led by a museum docent.

"Let's see if we can learn one new thing," I whispered to Emily, repeating a line often said by Claudia. She giggled and agreed, so we attached ourselves to the class, just like Claudia and Jamie did. We actually learned five or six new things before leaving the group to explore the temple on our own. Then Emily led the way into the adjacent rooms, where she flitted from case to case, sarcophagus to mummy, keeping up a nonstop commentary on what she saw: "Probably they had those little dolls and animals in the tombs to play with in case they weren't really, like, dead, or probably they would get to take them to heaven, because they probably had, like, magical powers, or probably . . ." and so on and so on.

At last, museum fatigue started taking its toll, but before heading to the cafeteria to recover, we took time to hide for a spell in the very same tomb that protected the Kincaids from discovery during one close call. We had no one to hide from, but that didn't bother Emily.

"What if we could hide here all day?" she whispered. "And if we could trick the security people? And if we could be here after it closed, and see if the mummies came alive?" She let that thought hang for a second, then decided it was all too creepy, and it was time to eat.

The Itinerary

If you really wanted to be authentic to the book, you'd start your trip in Greenwich, Connecticut, take the train to Grand Central Station, go to the Metropolitan, take a couple of brief forays out of the museum, and then hop a train back to Connecticut—to Farmington, to be precise, to look for old mansions like Mrs. Frankweiler's. We actually did take the Connecticut commuter train, but only because we happened to be staying with friends near Greenwich. Although every kid likes a train ride, and we enjoyed ours, it didn't add enough to a museum-going day to make it worth the trouble if you're already in the city. As for going in and out of the museum the way Claudia and Jamie did, don't bother—their main destination was Horn and Hardart's, the old Automat, which is long gone.

So, feel free to dispense with the extras and stay focused on the only destination that matters for this book: the Metropolitan Museum of Art. To get a sense of how Jamie's stinginess made for long, tiring walks, you could go to the Met on foot from Grand Central Station, but be warned that it's a trek of some thirty-six blocks, which is bound to lead to whining. (On the other hand, your child will probably love the awesomely vast Grand Central Station, particularly the ceiling painted with the constellations.) We started about fifteen blocks away, which was just long enough for short legs.

When you arrive, stop at the information desk, find a docent who knows the book (not all do), and ask for help. You'll be told, as we were, that the museum has made many changes since 1967. The exact fountain the kids bathed in is gone, as is the exact bed they slept in. As for Angel, the statue, well, that was the only fictionalized part of the museum. But there are similar fountains and a similar canopied bed, surrounded by reams of blue velvet, and some things remain the same: the tomb in the Egyptian Wing, the suits of armor in Arms and Armor, and the Costume Institute. There are also superb Angel-like statues in the European sculpture rooms. A *Mixed-up Files*–savvy information docent will help you plot a Kincaid course through the museum.

You'll probably start by heading back through Medieval Art (where Jamie stashed his trumpet case) to search for the bed; make sure to stop when something looks interesting, because kids can sometimes respond to beautiful things if they don't think they're "supposed" to be looking at them. Then you can wend your way through the rooms of European furniture, tapestry, and sculpture, seeking some statues from the Italian Renaissance. Next, move through Jamie's favorite area, the Arms and Armor section, and hang a left to go into the huge American Wing. Here you'll find a large, lovely pool and fountain, quite similar to the one the Kincaids bathed in. Instead of removing coins, let the kids toss one in.

From the American Wing, it's a short walk to the Temple of Dendur, which wasn't there in 1967 but which most kids love—and besides, it leads to the Egyptian Wing. You'll probably spend a lot of time in this area, between exploring the temple (and its fascinating graffiti), looking for the sarcophagus in which Claudia might have hidden her violin case (the exact one isn't known), inspecting the mummies, admiring the amulets, and hiding in the tomb. Given this area's popularity with New York City schools, you're likely to find a field-trip group to follow. The Costume Institute, which also gets a mention in the book, is in the basement.

When you've had enough, head through the hall of Greek and Roman art to the cafeteria, bypassing the table-service restaurant as an unnecessary extravagance, as Jamie would have.

Names and Numbers

The Metropolitan Museum
of Art
1000 Fifth Ave.
New York City
(212) 535-7710

www.metmuseum.org
Open Sun. and Tues.–Thurs.
9:30 A.M.–5:30 P.M., Fri.–Sat.
9:30 A.M.–9 P.M. Admission
free for kids under 12.

Hans Brinker or the Silver Skates
(1865)

BY MARY MAPES DODGE

Haarlem, Amsterdam, and Nearby Villages, the Netherlands

Although some Netherlanders resent this American classic because the author had never traveled to their country when she wrote it (and because it popularized the fictional but pervasive legend of the boy who stuck his finger in the dike), *Hans Brinker or the Silver Skates* is a remarkably accurate picture of Dutch life at a certain time and place. Because of global warming, the frozen winter world of the book has largely vanished, but thanks to the Dutch talent for preservation, you can make fair-weather visits to windmills, canals, and villages very like those Hans and his sister Gretel might have known. —SLT

This trip is ideal for families with readers between the ages of 11 and 14.

The Book

Ask around—although it's in print in many editions and easily found in most libraries, *Hans Brinker or the Silver Skates* turns out to be one of those books everyone's heard of and no one's read, except middle-schoolers who are assigned the book. The downside of that assignment, according to kids, is that the book "gives you a lot of info" or is "too much like a reference book." The upside is a melodramatic story of two poor but spirited children in 1840s Holland who find a miraculously skilled doctor to cure their father's amnesia.

Like other nineteenth-century books, *Hans Brinker or the Silver Skates* is sometimes too naive and sometimes too sophisticated for modern tastes. But, like other classics, it's more accessible in abridged versions, and it's a good read-aloud experience. The vivid characterizations and exciting scenes— life-and-death surgery in the living room! heart-stopping skate race action! snotty rich girls and warmhearted aristocrats!—are even more fun when acted out in your best parental hammy manner. The old-fashioned cheerfulness of the young people is a relief after too much cynical TV, and because ice-skating is an important motif throughout, it's especially fun to read in the winter.

Dodge based her descriptions of the Netherlands on interviews with friends about their childhoods in Holland, and as an American, she focused on national habits that she thought her readers would find exotic. She set her story in Broek-in-Waterland, a small village (based on a real-life, still-existing village) that Hans describes as a 5-mile skate on the river from Amsterdam. Today, it's a twenty-minute bus ride from that city.

Sixteen-year-old Hans and his 11-year-old sister, Gretel, live with their valiant mother and their disabled father, a once-vital dike worker who suffered a head injury years before and has since been an invalid, not recognizing them and unable to do anything but eat, sleep, and sit. The plot is set in gear by the announcement of an ice-skating race that will have as its prize a pair of silver skates. We won't divulge all the book's secrets, but parents of girls should know that Gretel is the real contender in the race.

Hans Brinker or the Silver Skates is full of surprises. It's certainly not a sedate ramble through a safely quaint, old-fashioned yesteryear. The earnestness of the educational parts only offsets a rip-roaring story that gallops through brain surgery, buried (and lost) treasure, a Rip van Winkle experience, a last-minute subplot of mistaken father-son estrangement, robbers creeping through the night, and, not least, the memorable race. Overall, it's an effectively told tale, because its beautifully drawn characters really give kids something to hold on to as they visualize that murky setting: the past.

The second fourth of the book is a travelogue that describes a two day skating adventure undertaken by some of the village boys. They travel from Broek to Haarlem, Leiden, and Amsterdam, taking some time to see the sights along the way and staying overnight once with relatives and once at an inn. This is the section that becomes a bit overburdened with facts, but it's also an important part of the tale. Imagine being able to ice-skate with your buddies from your small village to two big towns and then the biggest city in the country! This glory of movement and freedom is the more poignant for being unlike anything most kids can experience today.

By the way, the boy-with-his-finger-in-the-dike story deserves, we think, a little respect, in spite of its lack of factual foundation (which is what exasperates the Dutch). The legend may have predated Dodge, but her vivid telling gives the reader an unforgettable image of that cliché, "Dutch heroism in its battle against the sea." Considering the ravages of floods and the great loss of life that this small, below-sea-level country suffered as late as the mid-twentieth century, there's something to be said for a story that allows readers (young and old) to personalize an understanding of the dangers faced.

The Experience

"Look, skates!" shouted my daughter Patricia, 12, stopping her bike and pointing to an antique pair of wood, leather, and steel ice skates proudly displayed, along with other decorative artifacts, on the garden wall of the brick townhouse in this gentrified Dutch suburb.

"Ah, yes," said our guide, a gray-haired, professorial, and thoroughly informed woman. She turned her bike and came back along the path behind us. "Those are very old. You don't see those anymore."

"Do you have ice skates?" Patricia asked.

"Oh, not anymore. The canals don't freeze, nor even the rivers, most years. But when I was a child, in the 1950s, maybe even into the early '60s—oh, we skated all the time then! It froze every year."

"But it doesn't anymore?"

"Oh, no—the pollution, you know. The global warming. There used to be great ice-skating races, every year, from one town to another. But they can never plan them now. The water has frozen—once, twice? Maybe just once in the past ten years. My grandchildren have never gone ice-skating."

It was winter in the Netherlands and therefore cold and sometimes rainy, but we never saw a landscape of snow and ice. Such a scene would have been common in the seventeenth and eighteenth centuries, and indeed, we saw detailed representation of Dutch life on the ice during our visit to the famous Rijksmuseum in Amsterdam. We stood in the galleries near Rembrandt's *Nightwatch*, studying two small canvases with a hungry interest. Both *Winterscape with Iceskaters* by

Hendrick Avercamp and *River View in Winter* by Aert Van der Neer (both Dutch artists of the Golden Age) show a wintry but incredibly active world. The paintings each depict a little village in the country, where dozens of people are going about their everyday business—on the ice. On skates, or riding in sleds with ice runners, people are shown doing just about every sort of thing. Children play with hockey sticks, adults hold meetings and transport farm animals, and elderly women are pushed along in one-person ice vehicles.

When Patricia and I read *Hans Brinker or the Silver Skates,* I had explained to her that we might not see ice-skaters like those in the book, but until she spoke to the guide, I had not realized that the frozen world pictured in those paintings was gone—not just for a season or two, but forever. I have often expected, when we traveled, to talk to my kids about the changes wrought by time, about how transportation, work, school, and family life were different in the past. But I never realized that one day I'd be teaching them about climate change. It was a sad and sobering experience.

And it was an ironic experience, because Holland has battled so long against other forces of nature, and it has so successfully preserved the architecture and even the landscape of its man-made past.

In many ways other than winter weather, the world of Hans Brinker lives on in the preserved historic centers of the villages of Waterland, the canal-laced countryside area near Amsterdam. As we followed the trail of Hans Brinker, we found ourselves frequently in the company of Dutch schoolchildren—not because they were visiting sites mentioned in the book, but because they, too, were learning about the eighteenth and nineteenth centuries. In the parking lot at the region's wonderful living-history village, Zaanse Schans, for example, we were flanked on all sides by school buses. Kids were pouring out of the buses, laughing and chasing each other through the turnstiles and into the grounds. As Patricia and I paused to get our bearings and gaze at the magnificent sails of a half-dozen windmills rising into a cloudy sky, some of the kids headed into the modern, interactive Zaans Museum, home to artifacts from three hundred years of everyday life. Others followed teachers into the workshop of the *klompenmakerij* (wooden-shoe maker) or the cheese house. Others went into the tiny bakery museum. Meanwhile, residents who live in the historic houses of Zaanse Schans rode along the canal on bicycles, heading for the market or the office.

Zaanse Schans, created in the 1960s by moving historic buildings from various spots around the Zaans River area to one location, has restaurants, cafés, boat rides, bike rentals, and other tourist services in addition to its museums (both public and private). It offers the best of both commercial and noncommercial attractions for families. In one day, Patricia and I saw real windmills, still working—one grinding paint pigment, another grinding mustard—enjoyed a good Dutch meal, and rode bikes through the flat, watery landscape of the polders (reclaimed land parcels).

Patricia and I also went to some of the historic sites visited by the ice-skating boys, notably St. Bavo's Church, Haarlem's most important landmark. As the gray twilight deepened one afternoon, we approached the church, ready to go inside and see the monumental 278-year-old pipe organ that had been played by George Frederick Handel and Wolfgang Amadeus Mozart. To our dismay, St. Bavo's had closed early because it was winter. We knocked and knocked at the side entrance (it's no longer an active church), and finally a caretaker came and grudgingly allowed us in. "But no lights," she said. "We're closed. Just for a minute. I'm not supposed to do this."

There's nothing quite as cold as a massive airplane-hangar-size building dating from the 1300s. We remembered seeing little foot warmers in the museum, boxes that would be filled with hot coals and taken with the worshiper to church. Now we understood the need for such a thing. When we stepped into the enormous cathedral, gasping as the chill hit us and shivering in the gloom, we also gasped in awe as we gazed at the vaulted ceiling rising high above frescoed stone pillars. At the far end stood the organ, its 5,068 pipes impressive even in shadows. Truly, we had been taking the temperature of the past on this trip.

The Itinerary

Too many adults have told us that all they remember of their first trip to Europe was being marched through museums and churches that were incomprehensible and ultimately off-putting. But we well-meaning parents want our kids to grasp some of the significance of the past still so visible in Europe's cobblestone streets, towering churches, and half-timbered medieval warehouses. Holland solved this problem by making a unique commitment to living-history and open-air museums. Using *Hans Brinker or the Silver Skates* to plan a few major itinerary stops makes the travel even more fun and focused.

Because of Schipol Airport's fabulous on-site train station, it's a snap to head directly for Haarlem, a small, easy-to-negotiate city where the impressive historic center is also the main commercial area. You can stay in a hotel in the central district and take the train or bus, or ride bikes on various *wandelroutes* (walks) to several neighboring towns.

A rental car or bus will take you to Zaanse Schans for a day. If it's summer, you'll have lots of daylight, so you'll have time not only to visit the open-air village but also to rent bikes for an hour, as well as tour the wonderful new museum. The collection of working buildings holds kids' interest for two or three hours, as there are cheese-making and other demonstrations as well as full-size windmills to explore. Summertime brings canal boat rides as well. The fine shop offers terrific historic paper dolls, reproduction antique games, toys, and picture books in several languages. The adjacent, imaginative Zaans Museum, built in 1998, displays everyday objects from three centuries of local life. Walking a ramp that winds through the exhibits, visitors wear headsets that play an ever-changing soundtrack relating to the objects—some as big as boats, others as small as lace-making needles. Here you'll see all sorts of skates, gorgeous sleighs, and the ice sleds used to carry the old ladies along, as well as vintage ice-hockey sticks and other children's toys described in the book. There's an 1842 sledge with a scene commemorating a notable skating feat: when Claes Caescoper journeyed on ice more than 230 kilometers in one day to twelve towns in North Holland.

Just fifteen minutes east of the Zaans region is Waterland, where the village of Broek is located, as well as such well-known villages as Edam, where the medieval cheese market is re-created during summer months. These are charming locales, fun to visit and famous for their distinctive traditional dress and customs. But they're contemporary towns, too. History buffs on self-guided walking tours can explore the old town centers and seek out the unique architectural features, but with kids, bike rides through the region make the most sense. If you don't set out on wheels from Zaanse Schans, ask at the tourist office in Haarlem or Edam about bike routes. You'll receive printed guides and lots of advice, and you'll be steered to routes (all will be over flat land, remember) suitable for your family. We enjoyed an hour's bike ride between Edam and Vollendam that took us along a dike and through farmlands, from a cheese market to a fishing village.

After a few days in the country, when you're ready for the big time and head to Amsterdam, the best Hans Brinker–related stop is the Rijksmuseum (take the museum boat there if you can), home of Rembrandt's *Nightwatch* and other masterpieces. Don't try to explore the entire vast museum, a baffling rabbit warren of rooms filled with priceless paintings and the decorative arts of this world-ranging nation. Your goals are (1) the cool eighteenth-century dollhouses, which will give your kids an idea of the life of a child from a wealthy family three hundred years ago. These enormous models have incredible detail and luxurious craftsmanship, and they even reveal historic information that was not preserved in any other visual record; and (2) the two previously mentioned paintings by Hendrick Avercamp and Aert Van der Neer. They're hung in the most-visited and very beautiful galleries of the museum in a section centered around Rembrandt's *Nightwatch*. You can show the kids the ice-life paintings and stop at *Nightwatch* for yourself, sneaking a peak at some Golden Age still lifes and domestic interiors on the way in and out.

MORE DUTCH TREATS

The 1955 Newbery Award winner, *The Wheel on the School*, by Meindert DeJong, with illustrations by Maurice Sendak, is another gripping adventure story set in the supposedly quiet world of a Dutch village, this one in the northern part of the country. Still in print and widely available, it is a wonderful late-elementary book about six children (all the kids in the village!) who set out to find a wagon wheel for the schoolhouse roof, in hopes of luring nesting storks back to their village. Traveling families can go to the marvelous open-air museum in Enkhuizen called the Zuiderzee Museum to see a re-created fishing village like the one in the book. The houses were brought to this site, their late '40s and early '50s furnishings intact, from villages that were inundated at that time by the diking of the Zuiderzee. Not currently available in an American edition, but in print in the United Kingdom, is a picture book many parents will remember from their '50s childhoods, *The Cow Who Fell in the Canal,* by Peter Spier, illustrated by Phyllis Krasilovsky. It's a whimsical tale of a cow floating down a canal from a pasture in the country to the cheese market in Edam, and it depicts landmarks and buildings still visible in the Waterland region.

Names and Numbers

Netherlands Board of Tourism
355 Lexington Ave., 19th floor
New York City
(212) 370-7360
www.goholland.com

Zaanse Schans
Schansend 1, 1509 AW
Zaandam
(31) (75) 616 8218
www.zaanseschans.nl
Open daily 8:30 A.M.–6 P.M., till 5 P.M. Oct.–Apr.; Zaans Museum open Tues.–Sat. 10 A.M.–5 P.M., Sun. noon–5 P.M.

Rijksmuseum
Stadhouderskade 42
Amsterdam
(31) (20) 674 7047
www.rijksmuseum.nl
Open Tues.–Sat. 10 A.M.–5 P.M., Sun. 1 P.M.–5 P.M.

Harry Potter and the Sorcerer's Stone (1998) & Other Titles

BY J. K. ROWLING

London, Windsor, and Durham, England

No Harry Potter fan will want to visit London without seeking some of Potter's magic. Head to King's Cross Station to search for Platform 9¾, and take your own Hogwarts Express (a train from Waterloo Station) to the town of Windsor for a tour of Eton, the historic boarding school that evokes Hogwarts. And if you're traveling to the north of England, plan a stop at Durham Cathedral, which served as Hogwarts in the feature film—this is one church your kids will insist on seeing.

—CDB

This trip is ideal for families with readers between the ages of 8 and 13, but any children familiar with the books will have fun.

The Books

If you have a child between the ages of 5 and 15, chances are very good that you've read aloud, read along with, or had your child recount details of at least one of the four Harry Potter books. In fact, even if you're childless, you're probably pretty savvy about the 11-year-old English wizard who doesn't know

he's a wizard. Given the mania for this publishing phenome-
non, it's the rare person who doesn't have at least a passing
familiarity with Hogwarts and Diagon Alley.

In the first of the four books (which will expand eventually
to seven, says Rowling), we meet Harry. Orphaned in infancy,
he'd been sent to live with his horrible relatives, the Dursleys,
who make him sleep in a cupboard under the stairs. After
eleven years of friendless misery, his world turns upside down
when he is contacted by the Hogwarts School of Witchcraft
and Wizardry, informing him that he has been accepted for the
fall term. It turns out that he's been a wizard all along, the son
of a famous wizard and a witch, and the time has come for him
to learn how to fulfill his destiny.

All sorts of bizarrely fascinating characters come into his
life, and despite the Dursleys' angry protests, he is freed from
his cupboard prison and goes off to Hogwarts to learn wizardry.
Over the rest of *Harry Potter and the Sorcerer's Stone* and the
subsequent books, we follow Harry, his friends, and his ene-
mies through adventures galore, some comic and some quite
harrowing.

Not only is Rowling a ripping good storyteller, but she's
also blessed with a Roald Dahl–like British wit—the Dursleys
are as wonderfully rotten as the aunts in *James and the Giant
Peach* and the parents in *Matilda,* and when bad guys get their
comeuppance, it's often done with skillful comic timing. But
what immediately catapulted Harry Potter into the realm of
great kid-lit heroes is the blending of real boy and fantasy boy.
On one hand, he's a normal, candy-eating kid who can't control his hair and tends to be shy and cautious. On the other
hand, he has magic inside him that he never knew existed, and
as the books progress, he masters such thrilling skills as flying
on a broomstick, playing Quidditch (a magic form of soccer),
wearing an invisibility cloak, and casting spells on nasty people.

This is a powerful fantasy indeed for children, who so often feel powerless in a big scary world.

THE AUDIBLE HARRY

When travel plans mandate long car trips, consider buying or renting the Listening Library audio editions of the four Harry Potter books, available on either tape or CD. Each book is read by the British actor Jim Dale, who masters the many voices, the sharp humor, and the considerable suspense. Even after having read all the books themselves, our kids begged us to keep driving as we worked our way through the tapes. (We've known grown-up childless friends to sit in their driveways for ages, unable to stop listening!) And because the collection is unabridged, Dale reads it as Rowling intended.

The Experience

A few days before leaving on a family trip to London, we were telling friends in the school parking lot that we couldn't figure out how to have a Harry Potter experience. (Although the books have some London settings, most of the action happens in such imaginary places as Hogwarts, Gringott's Bank, and Diagon Alley.) Just then, 9-year-old Todd walked by and stopped. "You *have* to go to Eton," he said. "We went there last summer, and it was just like Hogwarts!"

Todd's advice saved the day. Ten-year-old Erin adored Harry Potter, and she was keen to do anything in the spirit of the books. We'd already planned to stop at King's Cross Station, where Harry's train departs for Hogwarts, but we knew that would be a short outing. So we also set aside an afternoon to see Eton College, the famed boys' boarding school founded in Windsor in 1440 by Henry VI. Eton was clearly a model for Hogwarts—they are both elite boarding schools for middle- and high-schoolers, with illustrious histories, tightly held traditions, and (one presumes) a plentiful supply of wealthy, sneering legacy students, à la Draco Malfoy, Harry's archrival. (The only difference is that Hogwarts is coed.)

After the sixty-minute train ride from London, we set off on a longer-than-expected walk from the station to the school, but no one really minded, because the town of Windsor was so fetchingly English. The great castle of Windsor, flags fluttering from its parapets, overlooks it all, giving the town a fairy-tale feeling, and we walked down cobblestone streets past shops set into ancient half-timbered buildings. The walk served as a good way to transition from the modern chaos of London to a slower, more timeless setting that primed the kids' imaginations and put us all in a Hogwarts state of mind.

When we arrived at Eton, the elderly ticket vendor took our pounds and told us, kindly but firmly, that we were to wait in the grassy courtyard for the tour guide and not go off exploring (Prince William was in his last year at Eton, and security measures were fairly tight). The place seemed eerily quiet. Through leaded windows on one end of the courtyard, up on the second floor, we could see a room of dazzling proportions, with vast beamed ceilings and significant chandeliers. "It looks just like the Great Room," saw Erin with awe, referring to the spectacular hall in which Hogwarts students and faculty met for banquets and occasions. "Only its ceiling probably doesn't turn into the sky," she added.

Our forty-five-minute tour commenced, and we trooped through the College Chapel (a hushed, serious place that Emily pronounced "magical"), the Cloisters, and a couple of ancient rooms in the Lower School, which seemed devoid of students, although it was a school day. The girls only half listened to our guide, a stiff-upper-lip sort who wanted to get through his routine about Eton's heavy history. We ended up in the Museum of Eton Life, where we inspected artifacts, pictures, and clothing from school life over the last half millennium. The tour concluded with a short film about daily life at Eton, and this really caught Erin's fancy. We'd yet to see any possible Harry Potters in person, but the film showed real boys in their daily lives here: studying, living in Gryffindor-like "houses," playing sports, conducting science experiments, eating in a grand dining hall . . . all the sorts of things that Hogwarts students did.

We emerged from the dark screening room into the School Yard, blinking from the sun—and saw boys everywhere, each in his Etonian garb: black striped pants, white shirt, black neckband-style tie, black jacket, and shined shoes. Erin and Emily were in heaven. And they were most impressed when a polite young black-haired student (like Harry, only taller) told us that this was just a break—even though it was after 5 P.M., they'd be back for more studies shortly. Whether one is learning to be a wizard or the next prime minister, life isn't easy at boarding school.

The Itinerary

Harry Potter goes to London with some regularity, typically to shop for school supplies (books, pencils, wands, potions) on Charing Cross Road. This is a very real street in the heart of London, just north of Trafalgar Square, and so it's likely that if you're doing the basic tourist rounds, a walk up Charing Cross will be easy to fit in. The only problem is that the Leaky Cauldron, the grown-up wizards' pub of choice (theoretically visible to Muggles—regular people—but somehow never noticed by any of them) on the street, is invented, as is the magical street of shops called Diagon Alley, which is entered via the Leaky Cauldron. But your family still might enjoy a stroll up the street, speculating about which pub could hide the entrance to a secret alley. And if you want to do a little shopping in the Potter vein, head for the Charing Cross Underground Shopping Concourse, near Charing Cross Station, where you'll find Davenport's, a first-rate magic shop.

The only other London stop on a Potter trip is King's Cross Station, where Harry and his pals boarded the Hogwarts Express. Only the right people can see it steam into Platform $9^3/4$, in between Platforms 9 and 10, and some kids get a thrill out of looking for it. (Erin and Emily weren't among them, declaring it boring, but their good friends Garret, 11, and Nora, 8, loved it.) Platforms 9 and 10 are off in a modern annex next to the vast old original station.

For a Hogwarts-like experience from a London base, plan a day trip to Windsor, the royal town reached via a one-hour train ride from Waterloo Station. Begun in 1070 by William the Conqueror, the castle itself is well worth a visit, especially (say the kids) to see Queen Mary's Dolls' House, surely the most incredible dollhouse in the world, built by fifteen hundred craftsmen over three years. Even the toilets flush. On the other end of town from the hulking castle is Eton College, first cousin to Hogwarts, which offers guided tours most afternoons. Try to visit when school is in session, because seeing the boys in their old-world uniforms is half the fun.

If you'll be heading to the north of England (say, for a Beatrix Potter visit to the Lake District), allow time for a side trip to the fine town of Durham, home to Durham Cathedral, one of the most impressive cathedrals in all of Europe. A UNESCO World Heritage Site, it's an amazing Norman monstrosity that has always been a mecca for cathedral buffs but has never been much of a hit with the under-13 set. All that changed when the cathedral was cast as Hogwarts in the *Harry Potter and the Sorcerer's Stone* feature film. (Other places around Britain served as bits and pieces of Hogwarts, but Durham was a key location.) With Harry, Hermione, Hagrid, and the many other memorable characters in mind, explore the cathedral, the impressive Monks' Dormitory, and the extensive grounds and side buildings, saving strength to climb the 325 steps up through the ancient tower. Keep an eye out for owls . . . and don't bump into any young wizards in invisibility cloaks!

Names and Numbers

British Tourist Authority
551 5th Ave., 7th floor
New York City
(800) 462-2748
www.visitbritain.com

Davenport's Magic Shop
7 Charing Cross
Underground Shopping
   Concourse,
Strand, Covent Garden
(44) (20) 7836 0408

King's Cross Station
Euston Rd. & York Way
Bloomsbury
(44) (8457) 484950 (national
   rail inquiries)

Eton College
Windsor, Berkshire
(44) (1753) 671177
www.etoncollege.com
Open daily late Mar.–late
Sept., with tours at 2:15 and
3:15 P.M.; closed some days
for special occasions, so
call first or check Web site.
Train runs every thirty
minutes from Waterloo
to Windsor and Eton
Riverside Station.

Durham Cathedral
The College, Durham
(44) (191) 386 4266
fax (191) 386 4267
www.durhamcathedral.co.uk

Open Easter–Sept., daily
10 A.M.–5 P.M.; Oct.–Easter
Sat.–Sun. 10 A.M.–4 P.M.,
closed Dec. 25–26.

Heidi (1880)

BY JOHANNA SPYRI

Graubünden, Switzerland

*L*ace up your walking shoes, study up on wild-flower names, and take the kids to Switzerland for fresh air, sunshine, bike riding, walking, and dramatic train rides. Today, as when Clara regained her health during a summer visit to Heidi's Alpine home, the region is a world-class center for outdoor recreation. —SLT

This trip is ideal for families with readers between the ages of 8 and 13 and their younger siblings.

The Book

Heidi is one of the most accessible of the classics for 8- to 12-year-olds. The characters—the Alm Uncle (or Alp Uncle, Heidi's grandfather), Peter the goatherd, Peter's grandma, the invalid Clara, the stern Miss Rottenmeier, the kindly doctor—are broadly and vividly drawn, quickly understood and immediately visualized. The situation—an orphan girl goes to live with her scary grandfather in an isolated Alpine hut, finds true happiness with him in the beautiful mountains, then is wrenched away to live among strangers in the bleak, gray city—is amazingly uncomplicated in Spyri's capable hands. And so the wonderful small details of daily life—goat's milk, toasted cheese, sleeping in straw, handmade chairs, fields of flowers—

take center stage. Those details are the keys that have unlocked generations of young readers' imaginations.

A solo reading of *Heidi* can be a most enjoyable experience for preteens, one that affords them hours of old-fashioned pleasure and an escape from contemporary life. They'll be in the company of an innocent, faithful, attractive young person whose troubles are solved in time by the efforts of people of goodwill and means. They'll identify with Heidi, who not only achieves happiness but brings peace and pleasure to others, while reconciling two troubled adults with their God. They'll be amused by Peter, a real guy—a monosyllabic outdoorsman who expresses love by scowling and who falls asleep when confronted by nature's beauty. And they'll indulge in the wonderful fantasy of having rich friends who are willing and able, when a need is pointed out to them, to improve the lives of the less fortunate.

But *Heidi* makes a nice read-to-each-other book, too, especially with grandparents. There are three wonderful grandparent figures, each rich and complex with personality, each loved by Heidi. The Alm Uncle, Heidi's grandfather, is one of the most memorable characters in children's literature. Embittered by tragedy and guilt, he has withdrawn from society and lives alone until Heidi is literally dropped on his doorstep. Heidi admires and emulates his competence and industry, his simple tastes and self-reliance. Peter's grandma, on the other hand, is a pitiful figure, huddling alone and blind in a dark corner of a shabby mountain hut, with never enough to eat or sufficient bedclothes to keep warm through the winter. But when she issues a simple invitation through Peter for Heidi to visit her, the child begins to form the social ties that eventually create a small, emotionally interdependent community right there on the mountain. In contrast, Clara's grandmamma is a confident, educated, worldly woman, full of good humor and wisdom, patient with children and powerful enough to influence events. She is vividly depicted riding up the mountain on a white horse, a guide before her and a porter behind her.

But, of course, as anyone who has read the book knows, the dominant character is the setting—and it is so important that a description of the path to the Alm Uncle's hut forms the first lines in the book. The glories of Heidi's home comprise one of the best-known lists of virtues in the world: crisp air, fresh goat's milk, wind in the fir trees, friendly stars, sweet-smelling straw, lush meadows, steep mountain paths, snow-capped mountains lit by the sunset as if on fire . . . it's a hard-hearted soul who can read *Heidi* and not immediately head for the nearest park to commune with nature. As one young reader said, "If you like the wilderness and peace and quiet, you'll love this book."

The Experience

Looking for Heidi's world in her home canton (or province) of Graubünden in Switzerland is as easy—and as satisfying—as walking off the pleasantly old-fashioned trains of the region and looking for the local walking trails. And that's very easy indeed, because the Rhaetian Railway (known as the "Little Red One") offers frequent service between the small, pictur-esque towns in the canton. And the trails, shown on detailed maps and marked with directional signs just like regular roads, seem to connect every village, viewpoint, mountain hut, and scenic wonder in the area.

Graubünden (as it's known in Swiss German—it's also called Les Grisons in French) is crisscrossed with these won-derful walking paths, many also used for biking. Eleven-year-old Patricia and I found some paths paved with asphalt and gravel, some that were dirt trails, and some that were simply mown strips through meadows (each community maintains the trails in its area). Before and after a visit to Maienfeld and Jenins, where Johanna Spyri vacationed and walked and may have dreamed up *Heidi,* we visited other parts of the canton. Wherever we went, it seemed, even when we weren't seeking them, scenes from *Heidi* in our minds were before us.

Partly that's because the landscape that Heidi loved so well, with its unobstructed views of snowy peaks and high-altitude meadows filled with flowers, is cherished by her real-life Swiss compatriots, who preserve the mountains as recreation areas, help keep rural communities alive through their own tourism, and support such marginal enterprises as mountain cheese huts.

And partly it's because certain aspects of life in the Alps are still organized as they were a century ago. In the winter, people and animals live in the valleys, in towns that are occupied year-round. In the spring, the livestock are taken to the valley's fields for fresh pasture after a winter of dry fodder. Then, in late May and early June (when the opening chapters of *Heidi* occur), the animals are taken to the higher mountain pastures. People go with the animals, first the herdsmen (who are often also cheesemakers), who have their own small seasonal homes, called huts; then the valley residents, many of whom might either have a hut or belong to a club that maintains one; and then the visitors, Swiss and German mostly, who walk hut to hut, viewpoint to viewpoint, village to village.

So in the hills above the town of Maienfeld and the village of Jenins, when Patricia and I went to see a museum called Heidihaus (Heidi's House) and then took the path designated as the one to Heidi's Alp, we didn't find ourselves on a trail any more or less beautiful than the others we'd walked on. But if Patricia had been a bit younger, it might have been a special walk for her because it features a kind of interpretive trail (like a touch-and-do nature walk) that also has signs with quotes from *Heidi*. (She'd also have been motivated to continue up the hill by the fun of looking for the next sign.)

At the top, we sat outside the summer hut of Luis Karner, a gray-bearded man employed for years by a half dozen Maienfeld farmers to watch their cows. The little sign pointing to Heidi's Alp owes its existence to the fact that so many tourists wandering around with *Heidi* in mind had found their way to Luis's hut and decided that he looked just like Heidi's grandfather.

"The farmers might prefer that Luis give all his attention to the cows, not the tourists," said a Swiss official I spoke to, "but even if we don't put the sign there, the tourists come!"

Just in front of the hut were two picnic tables, and Patricia and I were happy for a place to sit and have a cool drink after our two-hour uphill walk, which had offered us great views of the Rhine Valley, lovely wildflowers, and the chance to spot a chamois, a kind of small antelope. We sat looking at a panorama that took in snow-covered peaks, a green valley with the Rhine River cutting through, a number of villages—and a bunch of cows.

The herd was just a few feet away from us, in a pasture full of grassy plants that seemed so juicy we could feel the pleasure vibe from the four dozen or so grazing cows. It reminded us of how enthusiastic the Alm Uncle's goat is about the gourmet herbs she's fed so that she'll give particularly nourishing milk for Clara. Each cow wore a bell around its neck that clattered whenever the animal took a step or turned its head.

"But that's not noise," said Luis, raising his voice a little above the sound. "That's music."

It was music so particular to its place that neither Patricia nor I was likely to hear it again: each cowbell a different note, each note known to Luis. The bells were clinky, clattering, cutting through the mountain air.

Luis told us the names of the mountains we saw: Pizol, with its glacier; Calanda; Dreibündenstein (Three Gray Rocks), the historic birthplace of the canton. The snow on their massive dark shoulders was bright in the afternoon sunlight. "The cows are all ready to have their calves," Luis told us in quick, clear English. "As soon as one is ready I call the farmer on my cell phone and he must come and get her right away." We marveled at this mix of tradition and technology.

Then Luis showed us his ornate new pipe, presented to him (although he doesn't smoke) by friends who'd heard that some Japanese tourists had complained because he didn't have a pipe to hold when posing for pictures. He apologized for his beard being so short and explained that he and the cows had just come up the week before and he was still getting into character. I realized that I should take a picture so he wouldn't think we were disappointed, but Patricia was giving me her not-on-your-life look, so I'm now the proud owner of a souvenir photo of me with a guy who makes a pretty good Alm Uncle.

I knew I was tired when I patted my pockets for some of the glorious milk chocolate that had been fueling my walking and Patricia told me I'd already eaten it. How could I have forgotten eating something so good such a short time ago? So we headed downhill to the farm of Herr and Frau Just, where, in borrowed sleeping bags on fragrant straw, we slept the sleep that's at the center of the *Heidi* experience. Like Heidi, like Clara, we were refreshed by the still unbeatably health-giving and tranquilizing combination of mountain air, exercise, dairy products, and deep sleep.

The Itinerary

We don't usually recommend regions known primarily for their scenic wonders to traveling families. If you drive around looking out the car window, kids gets restless; if you try to augment the program with tourist activities, you find yourselves doing things (like miniature golf) that you might as easily do closer to home. But because of the quite reasonable distances between towns and regions in Graubünden (once you get there!), you can see some of Switzerland's scenic sights in a very *doing* sort of way.

If you begin and end in Chur, the canton's capital, you'll be in a small city with a pleasant pedestrian town center, good rail connections, and fine midrange hotels. The residential areas and schools are in and around downtown, so we felt at home with families with baby strollers, preteens on bikes, and young people everywhere.

From Chur, you can take the train or ride bikes (rented at the railroad station) along the Rhine to Maienfeld, where the tourist office has created the trail to Heidi's Alp and recently opened the Heidihaus museum. The brochures unfortunately tout this as "the original Heidi house," which it isn't (there having been no real Heidi), but guidebooks that are in a snit because the village in which it's located, Rofels, was renamed Heididorf (Heidi Village) have got it wrong, too. In fact, Heidihaus is a terrific hands-on, everyday-life museum, and it's part of a three-building hamlet that never was a village. Rofels's historic buildings were a cooperative rural Rathaus (town hall) and a farmhouse. Today, the farmhouse has become the museum, and the former Rathaus is occupied by a farmer-caretaker who tends to the goats and other animals on site. A new building houses a gift shop.

You enter the museum via tickets pushed into a ski-lift-style turnstile, and once inside—here's the good part—you encounter no guides, no tour, no "Don't Touch" signs. Furniture, clothes, tools, dishes, skis, and equipment from the nineteenth century were gathered from families in Maienfeld and arranged in appropriate rooms. Kids can try on Grandpa's clothes, lie in the beds, write on the slates, pretend to make cheese, look in the cupboards, and sit on the wooden privy. The Johanna Spyri Foundation provides a little library (one section under glass, one section open for use) of editions of *Heidi* from many countries.

So you'll find that Heididorf is modest as tourist attractions go, with its museum, goats (who may be fed), a shop, and an ancient stone water fountain. A walking path from the Maienfeld train station brings you there or, between May 12 and September 30, there's an hourly shuttle from the station. The tourist office provides trail maps and suggests routes of varying lengths. If you take the shuttle to Heidihaus and then walk up Heidi's Alp (Ochsenberg) to where we met Luis, it'll take about three hours round trip, and you'll have an elevation gain on the hike of about 1,500 feet. Add an hour in the museum, lunch, and some time to feed the goats, and you've filled up much of the day.

A mile away from Heidihaus at the foot of Faulkniss (one of the peaks mentioned in *Heidi*) is the Just family's dairy farm, where you can sleep in straw, Heidi-style. The Justs have converted one part of a farm building—cement floor, wooden walls, red geraniums in a window box—into a cabin in which more than ten can sleep, some on mattresses and some on straw. There's a motel-style bathroom and a table and chairs. Frau Just serves breakfast (and other meals) in another building. The farm (a dozen cows, some black-and-white speckled chickens, an orchard, fields, a brindle cat) is a popular stop on several major cycling routes, so the sleeping quarters are well booked in the summer. Kids can add their words and drawings to a guest book ("I was warm and happy") dating back to 1995.

Within a five-minute train ride or ten-minute drive from Maienfeld are Bad Ragatz and Malans, whose cable cars are a terrific family experience. Cable cars are found throughout the region, some functioning year-round to offer access to mountain trails. In Bad Ragatz, where Clara took the cure, you can enjoy a public spa complex of mineral baths, take a cable car to Paradiel, then walk a trail marked with illustrated *Heidi* storyboards to the Schwarzbüel Alp. The cable car in Malans has a restaurant at the top, staffed by volunteers (you eat whatever the nice lady makes that day—often something homey like *Aeplermagronen*, macaroni and cheese), and trails leading off to excursions that range from a half-hour loop to a hike to Italy. Reasonable family walking goals include a few lakes and (in season) a cheesemaker's hut where you can buy mountain cheese. (By the way, to taste what Heidi's grandfather served when he offered "meat he dried himself," buy or order *Bündnerfleisch,* or air-dried beef, a regional specialty. To enjoy an approximation of the "toasted cheese" he feeds Heidi, ask for raclette.)

Finally, you'll want to take one of the Rhaetian Railway's special excursion trains through the Alps. All leave from Chur or a stop or two away. Packages offer a train ride one way and a bus ride back that afternoon, but that's for folks who like to spend their entire journey in a vehicle looking out the window. The Glacier Express is the best known, a seven-and-a-half-hour journey to the Matterhorn. Travelers with kids should make the Heidi Express or the Bernina Express one wonderful leg of their trip. In four-hour journeys from the Chur area, both travel through beautiful valleys (often close enough to meadows to see individual wildflowers) and then into dramatic mountains.

The trains wind slowly up switchback tracks, then climb through the glaciers of the Bernina Pass, where Patricia and I thrilled to snowfall in June. Both go to Tirano in Italy, and the Heidi Express continues to Lugano. You'll want to go as far as Tirano (about four hours from Chur) to experience the moment when the train makes a complete circle on an elevated viaduct. After that (unless you plan to vacation in Italy), reboard and head back (twenty minutes) to overnight in Poschiavo, Switzerland, a small, picturesque Italianate town where you can eat pizza and pasta, swim in a nice public pool, stroll to nearby villages, and see hundreds of skulls in the ossuary.

When Patricia and I rode, there was a sense of excitement among the passengers. People from several countries stuck their heads (and cameras) out the windows, grinning at the scenery and gulping the lively air. Like Heidi and Clara in the mountain meadow, Patricia and I just sat and looked.

The sky was dark blue and not a single cloud was to be seen. The great snowfields overhead sparkled as if set with thousands and thousands of gold and silver stars. The two gray mountain peaks lifted their lofty heads against the sky and loomed solemnly down upon the valley as of old.

Names and Numbers

Switzerland Tourism
608 Fifth Ave.
New York City
(877) SWITZERLAND
(877) 794-8037
www.myswitzerland.com

Graubünden Vacation
Alexanderstrasse 24,
Chur, Switzerland
(41) (81) 254 2424
fax (41) (81) 254 2400
www.graubuenden.ch

Just Family Farm
(Sleep in Straw)
D. und M. Just
Bovelgasse 26, Maienfeld
(41) (81) 302 3841 (phone
and fax)
Open May 1–Oct. 31.

Rhaetian Railway
Bahnhofstrasse 25, Chur
(41) (81) 288 6104
fax (41) (81) 288 6105
www.rhb.ch

Swiss Travel System
www.sbb.ch
*The system offers a family
pass good on train, bus, and
boat that allows all children
under 16 to travel free if*
*accompanied by at least
one parent, providing a
significant savings on the
Bernina and Heidi Express
excursion trains.*

Hill of Fire (1971)

by Thomas P. Lewis
Illustrated by Joan Sandin

Paracutín Volcano, Michoacán, Mexico

Before Mount St. Helens, there was Paracutín, a volcano that attracted worldwide attention when it grew in a farmer's field in Michoacán in 1943. Lewis's simple telling of the volcano's birth from the point of view of the farmer's son has inspired many children to wish they could see a volcano for themselves. Travelers who head for this New World Pompeii will see a historic and scenic region, home to pre-Columbian ruins, famous craft villages, Day of the Dead celebrations, and a butterfly preserve.

—SLT

This trip is ideal for families with readers between the ages of 12 and 14, who read this book at an earlier age, and older siblings.

The Book

This unpretentious easy reader, with its carefully limited vocabulary, stripped-down narrative, and deliberately simplistic emotional content, doesn't pretend to be a classic. But because of its graceful prose, its unique position as a story set in Mexico but written in English, the effectiveness of its illustrations, and the awesome, real-life event it's based upon, *Hill of Fire* has been steadily read, in and out of the classroom, for more than thirty years.

The history of children's literature has a few dark chapters, of course, and one of those is the prevalence of racist stereotypes in so many works written prior to the 1960s. At that time, authors, publishers, and educators began actively addressing the need for interesting stories with more complex images of children of all races, creeds, and cultures. The result, over the decades, has been an upsurge in good-quality novels and biographies featuring American kids with a variety of ancestries, but most children's books in English about other countries tend to be fables and folklore collections. *Hill of Fire* is the rare twentieth-century storybook for English-speaking children whose characters live in a real, not imaginary, foreign country.

In fictionalizing a volcanic mountain's dramatic beginnings, Thomas P. Lewis does excellent work with time-honored storytelling tools. Because his writing and Sandin's illustrations have held up so well, thousands of kids have dreamed a dream of rural Mexico, living for a few days with the mental images of cataclysm and upheaval. It's not too scary to think "what if" about volcanoes after you read this book—and in a gentle way, it makes you wonder how you'd feel if your house and town were buried in lava. It's hard to imagine an easy reader (designed for ages 4 to 8) being the kind of book you remember twenty-five years later, but "Oh yes, I read that book!" and "Oh yes, I read about that little boy!" are common responses to a mention of *Hill of Fire*.

That's a special kind of contribution to make, establishing a personal, intimate connection that persuades a young, beginning reader to step through the pages of literature to discover the wider world.

The Experience

It was hot, of course, and the summertime Mexican sky was a brilliant blue. It was perhaps too hot to be standing there looking out over acres and acres of hardened black lava, jagged and uninviting in the middle of the fields, broken and dusty and powdery by the roadside. I took a swig of my orange soda and patted my brow with a cool, wet bandanna. I peered up at the cone of the mountain, trying to look at just the right time to see the silhouettes of my friend's sons Jeff, 12, and Dave, 11, who must certainly have been near the top by that time.

I was the monkey in the middle of our two-car group. Both cars had driven out from Morelia to the village of Angahuan to see Volcán Paracutín. One car, with parents and younger kids (including mine), had parked at the visitor center for an hour or so while its occupants looked at the exhibits and gazed with stunned disbelief at the towers of the lava-entombed cathedral. After they took plenty of photos, they headed off to a park of shady jungles, amazing flowers, and cool waterfalls. My car carried the intrepid Jeff and Dave, boys who were never more comfortable than when they were hot, dirty, and exhausted, boys who wouldn't miss the chance to climb to the top of a volcano, boys who had set out on rented horses, accompanied by (thank goodness) a guide, not me.

We had left the lovely colonial city of Morelia early in the morning, traveling on the main highway and stopping after forty miles for breakfast in Pátzcuaro, a small city whose vibrant indigenous presence is overlaid with faded colonial grandeur. (It's on the shore of the lake where the country's most famous Day of the Dead celebrations take place.) There we stepped into the Museo de Artes Populares, where we showed the kids the full-size example of the traditional wooden houses made by the area's Tarascan people. Dionisio Pulido, the farmer in whose field the volcano grew, was a Tarascan. We would soon see more of these cabins, called *trojes,* in the villages throughout the region.

From Pátzcuaro we continued on, past avocado groves and cornfields bordered by agaves, to the small village of Angahuan. About a mile and a half beyond the village is the visitor center, where the views of the lava fields, buried church, and volcano itself are fantastic. Guides with horses gather in this area to hire themselves out for either a half-hour ride to the church and location of the engulfed village or the four- to five-hour round trip to the rim of the caldera. Jeff and Dave had chosen the longer trip so that they could get up close and personal with a real (if dormant) volcano.

Of course, I couldn't see the boys on top of the volcano from my vantage point. I did hear later that they'd ridden across the plateau and a fair way up the cone but then finally had to dismount, tie the horses to shrubs, and continue on foot, scrambling in loose lava gravel. At the top, they looked into the vast dormant crater and beyond, seeing other volcanic peaks, some black cones like Paracutín and some older ones covered with trees.

"We ran down the volcano!" Jeff told me. "There was black sand in one part—it was fun, like running down a sand dune."

"You're taking big, huge steps all the way down," said Dave. "It's so cool. We couldn't stop laughing."

Before heading back to Morelia, we stopped in Angahuan's village center to see a different church, one that hadn't been threatened by Paracutín's eruption. It dates from the sixteenth century and has a fascinating triumvirate of carvings. The church doorway reflects the height of colonial artisanship with its ornate Arab-Andalusian-style carvings. Then there's a large courtyard cross, decorated with such pre-Columbian motifs as serpents and skulls. Finally, we found the modern sculptural treatment on one of the courtyard entrances that tells the story of the volcano. As in our storybook *Hill of Fire,* the tale told on this doorway ends with the arrival of tourists like us.

The Itinerary

A visit to Volcán Paracutín can be made as a day trip from the state capital of Morelia or as part of a stay in Uruapan or Pátzcuaro. The latter two towns are among the several destinations in Michoacán that are enjoyed for their historic architecture, colorful markets, excellent parks and natural attractions, and rich cultural traditions. Uruapan (about 75 miles from Morelia), for example, has cobblestone streets, lots of trees and flowers, and good hotels and restaurants. Its Museo Regional de Arte Popular is one of several well-regarded crafts museums in Michoacán, with impressive exhibits of Uruapan's own specialty, lacquerwork. Its *mercado* will give *Hill of Fire* readers an experience of an authentic market as depicted in Sandin's illustrations. (Because Sandin traveled to the region before creating her drawings, they contain specific and accurate details. The villagers live in *trojes,* the items for sale in a picture of the village market are appropriate, the kitchen utensils are correct for the period, and so on.)

Travelers who opt to stay in Morelia can make a day trip to Paracutín, and on other days head for an equal distance in other directions to Tzintzuntzán to see the terraces and temple ruins of the ancient Tarascan capital, or (between November and April) to the monarch butterfly preserves near Ocampo.

Morelia, a national monument and UNESCO World Heritage Site, is about halfway between Mexico City and Guadalajara on a connector highway to the superhighway between those two cities. There are direct flights into Morelia from some

American gateways as well as via Mexico City, and there is also an airport in Uruapan.

Guided day trips can be arranged through many hotels and local tourism offices.

Names and Numbers

Mexico Tourism Board
(800) 446-3942
www.visitmexico.com

Tourism Office Michoacán
(52) (443) 3128081

Island of the Blue Dolphins (1960)
BY SCOTT O'DELL

Channel Islands National Park, Ventura/Santa Barbara, California

The sun-drenched California coast is the jumping-off point for a boat trip to these enchanted islands, which are close enough to be seen from the shore, yet far enough away to have their own unique animal species. In an easy day trip, with no special preparations, you and your children can see life through the eyes of a castaway Native American girl of the early 1800s, and in the process encounter dolphins, whales, and many other creatures of the wild. —SLT

This trip is ideal for families with readers between the ages of 9 and 13 and older siblings.

The Book

Our island is two leagues long and one league wide, and if you were standing on one of the hills that rise in the middle of it, you would think that it looked like a fish. Like a dolphin lying on its side, with its tail pointing toward the sunrise, its nose pointing to the sunset, and its fins making reefs and rocky ledges along the shore. Whether someone did stand there on the low hills in the days when the earth was

new and, because of its shape, called it the Island of the
Blue Dolphins, I do not know. Many dolphins live in our
seas and it may be from them that the name came.

This beloved tale of a young girl who spends years alone on an island, surviving because of her intelligence and energy, like a young, female Robinson Crusoe, is based on a true story. Like other stories of children surviving in the wilderness, it is prized by educators and is required reading in many fifth- and sixth-grade classes, where it serves to illuminate Native American practices and history.

But this book's impact on young readers seems to be most profound because of the relationship the main character, Karana, has to wildlife. We asked some middle-school kids what they remembered about the book.

"I remember the animals," said my daughter Irene thoughtfully. "The dog named Rontu. It was a wild dog, the leader of the pack that killed her brother, and at first she was going to kill it, but instead she tamed it."

"And she had birds, too," said another child. "She had them live with her in a house she made of whale bones."

"And an otter. She had a pet sea otter!" chimed in a third.

O'Dell's imaginative leap—one that has kept the book in print for more than forty years—was to create a story that gave voice to the public's newly emerging desire to live on more peaceful terms with the natural world. He shows this desire forming in his heroine, Karana. Accidentally left alone on the island when her tribe is moved to the mainland, Karana is well versed in the hunting and gathering skills used by her people. Although there are no other humans, Karana sees life everywhere: sea lions and dolphins swim in the sea, birds fly overhead, and wild dogs terrify her. At first she kills the wild dogs and other animals to survive, but eventually, having befriended the dog, birds, and otter, she decides to live with them as she has learned to do—in harmony.

That change of heart has no doubt inspired three generations of park rangers, and the not-so-lonely world of *Island of the Blue Dolphins* seems like a kind of Eden for many young readers. It's not that they actually want to be cast away on an island and endure long, cold nights. But a glimpse of an otter they might befriend or a cave they could explore—now that is fun!

ABOUT THE CHANNEL ISLANDS

Established in 1980, Channel Islands National Park includes five of the eight Channel Islands that lie off the southern coast of California, and their surrounding one nautical mile of kelp-forested ocean. The ocean for six miles around each island is designated as a National Marine Sanctuary. Much of the scientific interest in the park arises from the isolation of the islands and the consequent uniqueness of plant and animal species. This concept, of course, is explained and symbolized in *Island of the Blue Dolphins*. The park is home to more species of seals and sea lions (pinnipeds) than anywhere else in the world, and the numbers of individual animals found here is staggering—between 180,000 and 200,000 at any given time. ✵ Anacapa is the nesting ground for the brown pelican, a species that's been brought back from the brink of extinction. In 1969 only one pelican chick hatched on Anacapa. Recent years have seen 4,000 to 6,000 breeding pairs of the majestic seabird. We encountered plenty on our trip.

The Experience

It was near the end of our day trip. The sky was darkening and gray. We'd spotted another whale after leaving the island, but now the skipper just wanted to get the boat back to port. Irene, my 13-year-old, huddled in her fleece jacket and rested her head on my shoulder. Suddenly one of the crew hollered, "Look! Dolphins!"

The cry echoed around the boat, but no one needed to point. As Irene and I rushed to the starboard side, we saw the water literally churning with dolphins. In every direction—port, starboard, fore, and aft—we saw hundreds and hundreds of glistening gray bodies, leaping in groups of six and eight, like a Sea World show in a hall of mirrors. We leaned over the rail to watch them ride the waves created by the bow, and then drew back in awe. Instead of one or two dolphins playing at the boat's bow, there were ten or fifteen on each side, jockeying for position. The skipper estimated that we were in the middle of a pod of two thousand animals.

A 10-year-old boy sat next to us, stunned and speechless. He was thinking, he later told me, of how he'd read about Karana in her balsa plank canoe, paddling through the dolphins. Now he'd seen the dolphins with his own eyes.

We hadn't known what to expect on our visit to Channel Islands National Park. Would it be like Hawaii or like science camp on Catalina Island? Would it feel different from being at a state beach on the mainland?

As it turned out, it was not an experience like any we'd had before, even in other national parks. Maybe it's most like going to a wild-animal park in Africa, because all day long we saw animals: two giant purple jellyfish, three gray whales, scores of seals and sea lions, a raft of cormorants, hundreds of pelicans, and thousands of dolphins. Our boatload of visitors was the only group landing on Anacapa Island that day. We realized that we humans were vastly outnumbered, just as Karana was. Karana found herself separated from other humans by miles and miles of water, but surrounded on all sides by wildlife.

The Itinerary

Either Ventura or Santa Barbara makes a good base from which to launch a family visit to Channel Islands National Park, and both beach towns are home to important museum exhibits on Native American culture (the Chumash and Gabrielino, or Tongva) that will enhance children's appreciation of the achievements of Karana in *Island of the Blue Dolphins*. And at Mission Santa Barbara, you can visit the gravesite of the actual woman Karana was based on (named Juana Maria by the mission fathers, although no one knows her real name), who died in 1853.

We recommend arriving early the day before your scheduled channel crossing and visiting either the Santa Barbara Museum of Natural History or the tiny pair of museums in Ventura: the Albinger Archeological Museum and the Ventura County Museum of History and Art. Irene insisted that both of these one-hour museum visits were worthwhile, because the Albinger exhibits fragments of pottery and other Indian artifacts ("They're really real"), and the Ventura uses reproductions and models to give visitors a detailed picture of tribal life. Museum shops sell O'Dell's novel and Chumash-design notecards, pencils, magnets, and the like. On the third Sunday of every month the Ventura County Museum offers family activities in the Chumash Discovery Center, with such hands-on activities as grinding acorns and making beads.

The national park's visitor center is on the mainland, at

Ventura Harbor, and boats to the islands leave from an adjacent dock. Visitor center exhibitions include a tide pool with a low side wall, so little ones can see into the rocky tank full of starfish, sea anemones, and sea cucumbers. There are other wildlife and paleontology exhibits, too. Various books and nature guides are for sale, along with trail guides for the islands.

Visitors can get to the park by private boat if they happen to have one, but most come on boats operated by park concessionaires. We took the day trip to Anacapa Island, the closest island and the easiest, most affordable, and most accessible excursion for first-time visitors. The all-day trip features an hour-and-a-half boat ride each way, during which whales (gray in the winter, blue in the summer) are sought and often spotted. The sea approach to the island is spectacular—you will see a beautiful arch formation, high cliffs, and many sea caves like the ones described in the book.

After landing, you can picnic and walk the easy mile-and-a-half nature trail along the plateau (with or without a ranger/naturalist guide). The island's hills are like those in the book, but there are neither trees nor water (there are two springs on Karana's island). However, there are different sights—from seagulls nesting on the ground alongside your path to hillsides covered with wildflowers—in different seasons. The sense of isolation is strong, especially to young minds, even though you can often see the other islands and the mainland shore. This small island fulfills every child's picture of an island, because you're on a plateau and can see down to the rocky shoreline, where sea otters and sea lions sun themselves. The kelp forests, frequently mentioned in the book, are also quite visible from this vantage point.

Kayaking (offered by the concessionaires in some seasons) around Anacapa allows you to relive aspects of Karana's adventures in the two sea caves she finds.

*The walls were black and smooth and slanted far up over
my head. The water was almost as black, except where the
light came through the opening. Here it was a gold color
and you could see fish swimming around. It was very silent
in there with no sound of the waves on the shore and only
the lapping of the water against the rock walls.*

In the summer, you can swim and snorkel from the boat or
a rocky beach.

Island of the Blue Dolphins pilgrims have other options
besides the full-day trip to Anacapa. You can do a half-day visit
or a half-day cruise with no island landing, either of which
(unless the seas are stormy) allows for plenty of wildlife sight-
ing. Other excursions will take you to Santa Cruz, the largest
of the islands at 24 miles long, with 10 miles of trails. There, in
addition to other wildlife, you might spot a Santa Cruz Island
scrub jay or an island fox (both unique species), just like the
blue jays and little red foxes in the book.

For experienced hiking families, a day trip to Santa Barbara
Island brings the chance to see the huge northern elephant
seals. You may not feel like you're on an island as much on
Santa Barbara and the other larger islands, but they more fully
duplicate the range of habitats described in the book. There are
also day trips to Santa Rosa Island, but we don't recommend
them for most families with young kids, as the crossing is three
hours each way. Determined camper-hikers can make the long
crossing to San Miguel and, after a fifteen-mile hike, see the
breeding grounds of sea lions, seals, and elephant seals.

Channel Islands that are not part of the national park
include famous Catalina Island, which can be a fun trip, but
because of the town of Avalon and a century of commercial
development, it is very unlike its sisters. Two others, San Nico-
las (where the actual woman on whom O'Dell based his novel

lived from 1835 to 1853) and San Clemente, are owned by the U.S. Navy and are not open to the public.

Names and Numbers

Channel Islands National
    Park
Visitor Center
1901 Spinnaker Dr.
Ventura
(805) 658-5730
www.nps.gov/chis/
Visitor center open daily;
closed Thanksgiving and
Christmas. Every Tues. and
Thurs. from Memorial Day
through Labor Day, a live
underwater video feed from
Anacapa Island can be viewed
at the visitor center or at the
Anacapa landing dock.

Island Packers
Authorized concessionaire
    to CINP
1867 Spinnaker Dr.,
Ventura Harbor
(805) 642-7688 (recorded
    information);
(805) 642-1393 (reservations)
www.islandpackers.com

TOURS: East Anacapa Island
All Day, departs 9 A.M.,
returns seven to eight hours
later; East Anacapa Express,
various departure times,
returns five hours later;
Anacapa Half-Day Cruise,
no island landing, available
Apr.–Nov., departs 9 A.M.
and 1 P.M., returns three
hours later.

Ventura Visitors and
    Convention Bureau
89 S. California St., Ste. C
Ventura
(800) 333-2989
www.ventura-usa.com

Santa Barbara Conference
    and Visitors Bureau
1 Santa Barbara St.
Santa Barbara
(800) 676-1266
www.santabarbara.com

Kidnapped (1886)

BY ROBERT LOUIS STEVENSON

Isle of Mull, Scotland

Stevenson named hundreds of Scotland's hills, mountains, valleys, and lochs in this classic adventure story, so using *Kidnapped* as a map would carry the traveling family through many, many, many miles of ruggedly beautiful landscape. Zeroing in on the Isle of Mull allows parents to share with their children the experience of profound isolation—without having to be kidnapped and shipwrecked. —SLT

This trip is ideal for families with readers between the ages of 10 and 14.

The Book

From his village in the Borders region of Scotland, 17-year-old David Balfour sets out for a village near Edinburgh to reclaim his father's estate, but his wicked uncle (who now claims the estate) has him kidnapped. After being held prisoner aboard a ship bound for the New World, David is shipwrecked on the Isle of Mull, one of the Inner Hebrides Islands. He almost dies but then makes his way to the settled part of Mull, where he rejoins a shipboard companion, Alan, a Jacobite rebel, and the two set off to journey back to Edinburgh. In an exciting series of adventures over many months, the two young men make their way through Argyll, the Highlands, central Scotland, and Fife, aided by sometimes-warring factions of Scottish clansman and running from English soldiers who occupy the territory.

Kidnapped is a kind of travelogue valentine to Scotland from Robert Louis Stevenson. Every place named is real; every detail of landscape was once accurate. (He wrote at the end of the nineteenth century about the period a hundred years before.) The adult literary pilgrim can take the novel and a map of Scotland and draw up a satisfying itinerary encompassing scenic and historic sites by following in David Balfour's footsteps.

But as we parents read *Kidnapped* with our kids (it's best read out loud together, even with older kids, because the archaic Scottish words and dialect must be puzzled out), we got caught up in the *story,* with its masterful portrayal of political differences and loyalties, its romantic sketch of the culture clash between the highlanders and the lowlanders, and its often comic, always dramatic scenes between the two protagonists. Stevenson populated the Scottish landscape, a magnificent backdrop, with vivid characters: a modest crofter (farmer) and his wife, a hidden clan chieftain, the duplicitous and scheming uncle. The action-adventure aspect of the book is thrilling, too—our heroes not only engage in shipboard hand-to-hand combat and survive shipwreck but also dodge regiments of redcoats, skirt castles held by bad guys, and send secret signals to allies.

Kidnapped is the source of much of the romantic imagery associated with Scotland, in the same way that Stevenson's *Treasure Island* is the origin of many a pirate cliché. It's often on reading lists in middle schools but can be enjoyed out loud with late-elementary-school kids, too. Keep a dictionary on hand—the action flows more smoothly if you take a moment to look up such archaic or local words as "dominie" (schoolmaster), "plenishing" (equipment), and "kirkyard" (churchyard).

The Experience

We hadn't meant to so closely duplicate David Balfour's first, humiliating experience on Mull. He, poor lad, knew as the ship went down that it had come around the island of Iona and was just off the coast of Mull. But when he swam ashore in a sandy bay, he found himself stranded on a mini island. After two grim, lonely, hungry days, he learned from a passing fishing boat that he was on a tidal islet and that during low tide he could walk to the larger island. Feeling foolish even in his desperate condition, he finally did so.

The first afternoon my daughter Irene and I spent on Mull was somewhat similar. Jet-lagged and exhausted after a transatlantic flight and a day's drive, I steered our rental car off the ferry, feeling triumphant because I remembered to stay in the left lane of what was at first a two-lane road. But twenty minutes later, Irene and I found ourselves driving straight down the middle of a very narrow single-lane highway, dodging sheep, chickens, and the occasional pheasant as we drove through brown hills, in and out of pine forests, and then for miles along desolate and beautiful coast. Once in a long while we'd see a car coming from the opposite direction, and then we (or they) would pull into the nearest of the occasional paved pullouts on the side of the road to allow the other to pass.

After an hour I began to wonder where we were, and after ninety minutes I realized I'd taken the wrong turn and that it would take as long to go back as it would to continue forward. And so, like David, we spent much more time than was necessary becoming acquainted with the wild, rugged side of the island. Also like him, we came to use Ben More, the island's imposing central peak, as a landmark and guide. And, like David, we eventually found sustenance and shelter. He was welcomed into a stone cottage with a turf roof and given oat bread, cold grouse, and "strong punch." We gratefully checked into our cozy B&B and enjoyed a similar repast.

The next day, eighth-grader Irene and I drove with Colin, the postman, as he made his three-hour round. There are about three thousand residents on the Isle of Mull, most living in the town of Tobermory. In Tobermory, there are cafés and stores and churches and schools. But in other areas of Mull, there are mere dozens of people living in many square miles. There are many, many more sheep than people.

We accompanied Colin on one of Scotland Royal Mail's 140 postbuses (actually station wagons or minivans), which are, in some remote areas, the only form of public transportation. Locals might ride with Colin from the village where he's based to the Ulva Ferry or to one of the holiday cottages along his route, and it is official practice to pick up passengers who hail the postbus at any point along the route. But tourists like us simply ride along for fun.

"You must see a lot of the island," I said to Colin as we settled into his red station wagon with the Royal Mail insignia on the door.

"Aye," he responded in the musical voice of those who have Gaelic for their first language. "It's the same places, though, every day. Every day, twice a day."

And so we set off, leaving the village behind. We headed for the coast, past acres of gloriously blooming yellow Scotch broom, following the curve of Mull's eccentric winding road.

Each time we passed a car, the other driver would invariably stop and stick his head out the window to exchange greetings and news.

"So is the parson coming today, Colin?" asked one woman, who apparently hadn't gotten the news yet about who was on the morning ferry.

"Aye."

Or, later, from a housewife on her way to a far-flung neighbor's, "I was expecting some plants, are they not there yet?"

"No, not yet."

Colin had a box of groceries for one house and some mail for a cottage beyond. He put mail and some community notices in a box at the bottom of a long driveway, and mentioned that he worried about the elderly couple who lived in that house. Their view out across the sea was unparalleled, but he thought their situation was very lonely, especially in winter.

Newspapers and letters went into boxes at small sheep farms.

"What do you call those sheep with the black faces?" Irene asked Colin.

"Black-faced sheep," said he.

And so we drove along at twenty-five or thirty miles per hour, the sea on one side of the road, sheep pastures or cliffs on the inland side. Irene kept up a volley of questions, charmed by Colin's islander voice and entertained by his simple description of each household along the route. We weren't walking, as David Balfour had done (thank goodness), but the views outside the postbus window were just like the descriptions in the book: foothills covered in Scotch broom, more islands rising on the watery horizon, and here and there an isolated white-washed cottage with a plume of smoke rising from the chimney.

"Fierce" is a word used by Scottish cooks to describe high heat in an oven. It doesn't carry a hostile or negative connotation; it doesn't comment on the stove's motives for burning bright and steady and strong. Nor is it a term of awe. It's just the fact. Many elements of life in Scotland are fierce. The landscape is fierce, no question. There are green pastures, it is true, and they're dotted with sheep, but they're always backed by some megalithic peak of unusual shape and unknowable aspect. And just like in some other parts of the world (Hawaii, for example), each rugged peak and each breathtakingly beautiful cliff that plunges to the sea seems a holy place, known to the gods long before it was known to man.

Is all this wasted on children? Of course not, but they need to have something in the foreground to hang on to while, bit by bit, they absorb the grandeur of such a background. That was the beauty of our visit to the Isle of Mull. We put ourselves into that fierce landscape, but we had plenty to hang on to, thanks in part to *Kidnapped*. Black-faced sheep, island accents, small cottages, scones, and tea—all were easily within a child's frame of reference and scale.

The traveler's way onto and into Mull—by ferry, one-lane road, and postbus—is easy, fun, and almost folksy. The quickness with which you leave the big-town civilization of the mainland, pass through the rural, small-town hub of the island, and suddenly find yourself "out there"—miles from a mailbox, much less a telephone—is amazing.

When Stevenson chose Mull as a shipwreck site he was selecting not simply a rugged coastal setting but also a staggering landscape whose proportions dwarf human endeavor. He gave his heroes a humbling beginning to their journey. Even today, Mull becomes a potentially treacherous wilderness just a few miles from the ferry landing, where scores of holiday merrymakers and tourists come onto the island. Hikers can become lost on the snow-covered paths of Ben More; drivers can grow weary of the miles of unlighted one-lane road. What Stevenson so brilliantly conveys when shipwrecked David Balfour almost dies of exposure while fishermen pass by not far away, unaware of his plight, is how rural folk play the edge in terms of survival at the border of wilderness.

The Itinerary

To see the world of *Kidnapped,* we ignored the step-by-step of the hero's journey. It would have carried us in a rental car along hundreds of miles of narrow, winding mountain roads, driving on the left side. Our nerves would have shattered and our kids would have rebelled before we reached the sites of the historic Highland uprisings. Instead, we explored several of the book's settings within a day's drive of Glasgow and Edinburgh, and we discovered that the Isle of Mull is a rewarding family destination that allows travelers to experience not only the literal settings but also the spirit of the vivid tale.

From Glasgow airport we drove to the coastal town of Oban in about half a day, stopping only for fresh-baked scones and strong tea at a wonderful café called the Coach House in the amazingly picturesque village of Luss, on the shores of Loch Lomond.

Oban is a bustling center of ferry travel to the Hebrides, and it has a pleasant promenade of shops. Irene, who knew something about the significance of tartans from reading *Kidnapped,* realized we were in the region called Argyll and promptly bought some socks. The car ferry was great fun—just the drive into the car deck, the chance to explore the passenger decks, and the opportunity to get chips and sodas at the snack bar is a day's adventure enough for young kids. Older kids will notice some amazing sights, including crenellated castles, from the huge ferry windows during the hour's passage.

Mull is 24 miles long and 26 miles wide, but it takes much longer to drive its length and width than those numbers suggest. The ferry from Oban lands in the village of Craignure, and the main town, Tobermory, is about 20 miles away. We stayed part of the time in countryside B&Bs and part of the time in Tobermory, where our hotel was among several in a crescent of brightly painted commercial buildings looking out over the harbor.

David Balfour leaves Mull on a fishing boat, saving, even in that distant past, "a long day's travel and the price of the two public ferries." We, like other visitors, instead sought out yet another ferry ride, this one from the village of Fionnphort on the other side of the island from Craignure. It took us on an excursion to the islands of Iona (where St. Columba brought Christianity to Scotland in the sixth century) and Staffa (where the basalt columns of Fingal's Cave awed Queen Victoria, Mendelssohn, Tennyson, Keats, and many others before us). We also enjoyed our time in Tobermory, our base for a visit to Torosay Castle and a whale-watching cruise.

MORE JOURNEYS ON THE *KIDNAPPED* ROUTE

For real *Kidnapped* enthusiasts, here's a quick survey of other sites relating to the story: ⚔ The boys pass through several areas that were rugged then and remain so now, including such historic sites as Glencoe, today a National Trust area with a visitor center, hiking, and mountain climbing. They then cross Rannoch Moor, which can be seen from the Glencoe ski area and other mountains to the west, and which is reachable from the east from the mountain resort area near Pitlochry. ⚔ Later, the boys emerge from the moor and cross the Central Highlands, looking for a way across what was then a well-guarded boundary line. Along this line today are many historic castles and military sites that were land-marks even when Stevenson wrote. There's a vivid passage in the book where the boys look up at Stirling Castle, and a scene where they try to cross the Stirling Bridge but are turned back by a sentry. We recommend a stop at the old bridge (a surprisingly unprepossessing but authentically antique stone bridge across the water with one foot in a park) and a look at the castle from a distance, but we don't suggest a tour of the castle itself, which combines the worst of thoughtless modernizing with dull museum-making. Instead, be sure to take a day in Edinburgh for a tour of Edinburgh Castle, the pride of the Royal Mile, a UNESCO World Heritage Site. Like a small city in itself, the castle conveys the reality of Royal Scotland with its imposing state rooms and apartments, collections of armor, and such exhibits as the memorable Crown Jewels and Stone of Destiny, which are nestled together on velvet. ✕ Between Stirling and Edinburgh, stop for a few hours in Culross, a seventeenth-century town that our heroes mention only in passing but which fate, in the years since Stevenson wrote, has caused to be preserved in almost its original form. Walking the streets of Culross, with its gabled houses, yellow mansions, and proud kirks, is like walking with your kids through a 3-D stage set for all the town scenes in the book.

Names and Numbers

Scottish Tourism Board
23 Ravelston Terrace
Edinburgh
(44) (131) 332 2433
www.visitscotland.com

British Tourist Authority
551 Fifth Avenue
Suite 701
New York City
(877) 899-8391
www.travelbritain.org

Argyll, the Isles, Loch
  Lomond, Stirling and
  Trossachs Tourist Board
Old Town Jail, St. John St.,
  Stirling
(44) (1786) 445222 (for Mull
  and Stirling)
www.scottish.heartlands.org

National Trust for Scotland
28 Charlotte Square
Edinburgh
(44) (131) 243 9300
www.nts.org.uk (for Culross)

Edinburgh and Lothians
  Tourist Board
3 Princes St.
Edinburgh
(44) (131) 473 3800
  (for Edinburgh Castle)
www.edinburgh.org

Royal Mail Postbus Services
7 Strothers Lane
Inverness, IVI IAA
www.royalmail.co.uk
(44) (121) 465 4629

Linnea in Monet's Garden (1985)

BY CHRISTINA BJORK

Illustrated by LENA ANDERSON

Paris and Giverny, France

*E*very devotee of Impressionist art dreams of finding his or her way to France, where the movement was centered and where many of its masterpieces remain. Linnea is a Monet- and garden-loving little girl whose dream of visiting France comes true, and her enthusiasm for Paris, Giverny's gardens, and Monet's paintings is likely to inspire any child headed for France.

—CDB

This trip is ideal for families with readers between the ages of 8 and 11, and older siblings would also enjoy the outings.

The Book

Just think—I've been in a famous artist's garden! And I've been in Paris!

So begins this effervescent book, which combines a child's travelogue with art history and art appreciation. The narrator and protagonist is black-haired, rosy-cheeked Linnea, the heroine of a series of Swedish books by the same author and illustrator; *Linnea in Monet's Garden* is the one of the series that has gained enduring popularity in the United States and Britain.

Linnea (who seems to be about 8 or 9 years old) adores flowers and gardens, and she also adores her neighbor, a retired gardener named Mr. Bloom. After many visits to his apartment, when she pores over and practically memorizes a book about Claude Monet's Impressionist paintings, the two friends, young and old, decide to visit Paris and Giverny together, to see Monet's paintings and home firsthand.

Every minute of their journey is a thrill to Linnea, and her enthusiasm is sure to rub off on most children who are headed to France. (It can be read alone by most fourth-graders on up, and is a good read-aloud for younger kids.) The creaking wooden floor of the ancient hotel where they stay in Paris, the pampered Parisian dogs, the famous paintings in the museums, the amazing flavors of the French cheeses, the first sight of Monet's pink house . . . it's all new, and it's all exciting. Linnea and Mr. Bloom encounter minor disappointments, as all travelers do—their plan to ride bikes from the train station to Monet's house is thwarted, as is their plan to picnic by Monet's famous bench—but they always adapt and carry on. This flexibility and cheerfulness in the face of setbacks is a lesson that all travelers, not just children, can always stand to learn again.

The art parts of the book are told from the perspective of a 9-year-old girl, which means they don't bog down in boring grown-up detail. When Mr. Bloom explains Impressionism to Linnea, she gets it, and so do young readers. When Linnea explains how and why Monet painted the way he did, she conveys a lot of information in a simple, interesting way. And when she is unhappy with her own drawing of a water lily, she takes comfort in Monet's famous discontent:

> *But then Monet was never satisfied with his pictures either. Sometimes he was so dissatisfied that he would take a whole pile of paintings and burn them out in the garden.*

That's something with which many frustrated young artists can relate.

Late in the book, Linnea takes a breather from her travelogue to explain Monet's life, and because she emphasizes his family life, his eight children and stepchildren, and daily life in Giverny, the stories are interesting to kids.

The rich illustrations—Lena Anderson's original watercolors, reproductions of Monet's paintings, and photographs of the garden and his family—add tremendously to a child's enjoyment of the book. The more your child pores over the pictures, the more he or she will get out of the real-life experience later.

The Experience

Unusual circumstances had resulted in a long day of difficult car travel to get to Giverny. By the late afternoon, when my family drove into the pretty little village, we were all exhausted, and Erin and Emily had fallen asleep in the backseat. At least, we hoped, arriving so late (ninety minutes before closing) would mean sparse crowds. But then we saw the array of tour buses lining the narrow street along the Seine, and our hearts sank. How could the girls have a Linnea experience in the middle of a mob?

Amazingly, they had a wonderful time. Yes, it was crowded, and no, they didn't get to stand on the Japanese bridge all by themselves, like Linnea did—but the garden and house were exactly as described and pictured in the book, and the kids clearly had picked up Linnea's enthusiasm.

At the entrance to the property, we threaded our way through the busloads of tourists, mostly from America but also from Japan, England, Canada, and Germany, to get past the huge gift shop and into the garden. The girls were most anxious to find the water lilies, but we promptly got lost, and they decided instead that we should see the family's house—even though Linnea had warned them that the former children's rooms were not open to the public. We joined a throng and walked slowly through living rooms, past the wonderful collection of sixteenth- and seventeenth-century Japanese art, up to the bedrooms, then down to the only two rooms the kids liked: the vibrant yellow dining room ("You'd need a table that huge with eight children!" said Erin), and the kitchen, home to an amazing row of polished copper pots ("You'd need that many pots to cook for eight children!" said Emily). All in all, though, they decided the house was a bust. "I think it's pretty stupid to not let people in the kids' rooms," said Erin, who came to Giverny fascinated with Monet's family life and brood of children.

Then we headed into the garden, which was shouting with color in early July. Down by the lily ponds there was the expected crowd, but we kept walking, crossing one of the bridges to reach the edge of the property. As with so many adventures in life, we found that it isn't hard to shake humanity—just go a little farther, and you're likely to be left alone. So we found a quiet, people-free corner of the grounds, where the girls explored the creek that the Monet kids fished in, and we talked about what it would have been like in Monet's day. They decided that the Monet children were very lucky indeed to have such a garden in which to play, such a creek to fish, such a pond in which to row. We wandered through every inch of the property, and even when we rejoined the crowds, the girls were gleeful to find the landmarks they'd learned about from Linnea: the Japanese bridge, the faded blue rowboat, and, of course, the water lilies, which were every bit as lovely as we'd imagined.

Finally, it was into the inevitable gift shop, where we jostled for position with seemingly the entire population of London. Happily, the level of merchandise was high—no Monet lava lamps or "I Went to Giverny and All I Got Was This Stupid T-shirt" T-shirts—and the girls were terribly pleased with their Monet calendars.

As we recapped our day over an ice cream in a village shop, Erin declared the garden to be a huge success. "You should tell people to come here, because it's exactly like the book," she said. "Usually places aren't *exactly* like the book."

The Itinerary

This is an itinerary that most grown-ups will find pretty easy to swallow. You should start in Paris—to be precise, you should start by settling into a small hotel on the Left Bank. You can even stay in the same hotel that Linnea and Mr. Bloom did: the Esmeralda, a romantic, if rather threadbare, seventeenth-century hotel in a great Fifth Arrondissement location near the Seine. (We opted for the somewhat more upscale Hôtel Left Bank Saint-Germain, because it had a rare four-person family room at a fair price.)

After spending a little time exploring your hotel and neighborhood, the way Linnea did, it'll be time to head out to the

Marmottan. Because of the typical kid rhythm and the typical kid aversion to art museums, we'd advise making the trip first thing in the morning, when everyone's fresh. It begins with an always entertaining (for kids) Métro ride to the Sixteenth Arrondissement, to seek out this lesser-known nineteenth-century former residence, now a museum devoted primarily to the works of Claude Monet and his contemporaries. You'll pass the verdant, playground-studded Jardin du Ranelagh on the short walk to the museum, but don't stop yet—it's perfect for a blow-off-steam visit after you leave the quiet of the museum.

(One note before visiting the museum: It tends to be terribly overheated, and this being France, there are no drinking fountains, so stick a water bottle in a purse or backpack for the kids.)

First, head to the top floor to see a good sampling of Monet's paintings, along with a small, choice selection of works by his colleagues of the time, including Renoir. Then work your way downstairs. Our kids were bored by the middle (ground) floor, home to a hodgepodge of nineteenth-century art and antiques, so we quickly prepared to head downstairs into the Giverny collection by initiating a contest: See who could find the boat painting first, then who could find the painting with two water lilies. The game helped them focus on the works they'd become familiar with in the book . . . and the places they'd see in Giverny.

Finally, encourage everyone to sit a spell on a bench to just be with the famed paintings of the Japanese bridge, the water lilies, and the light. Once it's all sunk in, you can hit the park outside, then stop for lunch at either of the two good restaurants on the rue Chaussée de la Muette, La Rotonde, or Le Parc de la Muette, both of which have *menus enfants* (kids' menus).

Not every family will be up for a second museum visit, but if time and interest allow, you could follow Linnea's footsteps to the famed Musée d'Orsay, home to many great Impression-ist works, including some of Monet's—but if you really fol-lowed her footsteps, you'd walk right past the Orsay. (She and Mr. Bloom find terrible crowds and decide not to wait in line.) They land up instead in the basement of the Orangerie, sitting on the circular bench, surrounded by Monet's famed giant water-lily painting. Try to find an hour to have that experience.

After seeing Monet's work, you'll want to head for his for-mer home. The trip to Giverny is a full day's outing from Paris and involves a forty-five-minute train ride from the St-Lazare station to Vernon, the closest town (Giverny is a tiny village). From Vernon, a short cab ride across and along the Seine River will take you to the Monet house. (Coming via train is far preferable to driving, even if you have a car—the drive through Paris traffic can be horrific. Trust us. We learned the hard way.) Allow a couple of hours to explore the property (and the gift shop), and figure in time for a meal or pick-me-up in the village afterward, before returning to Paris.

Names and Numbers

Hôtel Esmeralda
4, rue Saint-Julien-le-Pauvre,
　　5th Arr.
(33-1) 43.54.19.20

Hôtel Left Bank Saint-
　　Germain
9, rue de l'Ancienne
　　Comedie, 6th Arr.
(33-1) 43.54.01.70

Musée Marmottan
2, rue Louis-Boilly, 16th Arr.
(33-1) 42.24.07.02
Métro stop: La Muette
www.marmottan.com
Open Tues.–Sun. 10 A.M.–
5:30 P.M.

Musée d'Orsay
1, rue de Bellechasse,
  7th Arr.
(33-1) 40.49.48.14
Métro stop: Solferino
Open daily except Mon.
10 A.M.–5:45 P.M. (Thurs.
to 9:30 P.M.)

L'Orangerie
Tuileries, place de la
  Concorde, 8th Arr.
(33-1) 42.97.48.16
Métro stop: Concorde
Open daily except Tues.
9:45 A.M.–5:15 P.M.

Musée Claude Monet
84 rue Claude-Monet
Giverny
(33-2) 32.51.94.65
Train stop: Vernon
Open Apr.–Oct. Tues.–Sun.
10 A.M.–6 P.M.

Little House on the Prairie (1932)
&and Other Titles

BY LAURA INGALLS WILDER
Illustrated by GARTH WILLIAMS

De Smet, South Dakota

*B*y the time the Ingalls family reached this frontier settlement in the Dakota Territory, they'd lived in a covered wagon, a dugout, a log cabin, and various shanties. Ma had had enough of this harsh, nomadic life, so they settled for good in De Smet, and Wilder set five of her nine Little House books here. Today, at the Ingalls Homestead, young visitors can play in a hayloft, make rope, ride in a covered wagon, dress in period clothes, and have a lesson from a real schoolmarm in an 1880 schoolhouse.   —CDB

This trip is ideal for families with readers between the ages of 7 and 11, but children of all ages will enjoy the experiences.

The Books

A long time ago, when all the grandfathers and grandmothers of today were little boys and girls or very small babies, or perhaps not even born, Pa and Ma and Mary and Laura

and Baby Carrie left their little house in the Big Woods of
Wisconsin. They drove away and left it lonely and empty
in the clearing among the big trees, and they never saw
that little house again.
They were going to the Indian country.

In 1931, Laura Ingalls Wilder, then in her mid-60s, published a novel for children based on her life as a pioneer girl in Wisconsin. *Little House in the Big Woods* was such a wild success that Wilder answered her fans' pleas and set about writing the further adventures of Laura and her family: Ma, Pa, big sister Mary, and little sisters Carrie and Grace, as well as a boy named Almanzo Wilder and a cast of supporting characters. The result was *Little House on the Prairie,* which details the Ingallses' covered-wagon trip west and their year in the Indian Territory (what is now Kansas). Next came *Farmer Boy,* about Almanzo Wilder, who eventually grows up to become Laura's husband; *On the Banks of Plum Creek,* which takes place back in Wisconsin, where the family returns after trouble in Kansas; and, finally, five books (starting with *By the Shores of Silver Lake*) set in De Smet, South Dakota, where the roving Ingalls family makes a permanent home.

Wilder's nine just-barely-fictionalized books went on to sell an estimated fifty million copies and inspire a successful 1970s TV series (based only loosely on the books), and they remain strong sellers today—in fact, many a midwestern school builds them into the curriculum for third- to fifth-graders. (Wilder's straightforward, declarative sentences and simple vocabulary make these long chapter books quite readable for 9- to 11-year-olds, and they're also fine read-alouds for kindergarten on up.)

Because the stories largely involve girls, the Little House books have long gotten an unfair rap as being "girl books," so boys generally refuse to read them. But we know rough-and-tumble guys who got hooked when the books were read aloud. Oh, sure, in the last three books the maturing girls spend far too much time on clothes, hair, and courting for any self-respecting male, but the earlier books, especially *Little House on the Prairie, Farmer Boy* (a boy's book anyway), *By the Shores of Silver Lake,* and *The Long Winter,* are filled with adventure and action: howling and circling wolves, fierce Indians, roaring prairie fires, wild pony rides. The drama is abundant. Will Jack the dog make it across the raging river? Will the family recover from the horrible "fever 'n' ague" (malaria)? Will Santa Claus find them on the desolate prairie? Will Almanzo make it through the blizzard to bring food to the starving townspeople? Many a reading-aloud parent and teacher has been begged for "just one more chapter," to find out what happens.

As Laura grows, she witnesses the growth of the United States, for better and worse. She describes the unspoiled prairie: "grasses blowing in waves of light and shadow across it, and the great blue sky above it, and birds flying up from it and singing with joy . . . and on the whole enormous prairie there was no sign that any other human being had ever been there." She recounts, from a child's perspective, the white settlers' plowing under of this great prairie. She tries to understand why her mother is so afraid of Indians while her father respects them. And throughout the books, even as a very little girl, she is torn between the longing for travel and adventure and the longing for a home. Part of the timelessness of the Little House books is due to that very conflict, with which so many children can identify. And the joy of the books is that they are so rich in both—each book details adventures galore *and* the happy comforts of home, comforts that are all the more cherished when life is so hard.

The Experience

"Good morning, children," said the white-haired teacher in a calico dress. "Laura, let me feel your hand."

Erin, wearing a bonnet on her head and a pinafore over her T-shirt, put out her hand obligingly.

"Oh, I feel how cold it is!" said Mrs. Cramer, the teacher. "That's what happens when it's zero degrees out and you just walked two miles to school. Before our lessons, let's have a warming-up march."

It was actually 68 degrees out, a glorious late-spring day on the Dakota plains. Erin and Emily had joined a few other children in the 1880 schoolhouse on the grounds of the Ingalls Homestead. They'd donned period clothes and taken their seats at 120-year-old desks, listening raptly to Marian Cramer, a music teacher and history buff from a nearby town who spends her summers as the Homestead's living-history schoolmarm.

So they warmed up by singing "Yankee Doodle" and marching around the schoolroom. Cramer assigned each of the children a name based on the characters in the Little House books: Laura, Mary, Carrie, Grace, and their boy cousin, Jean. (Emily was assigned Mary, and she instantly went into character, staring off in the distance with wide-open eyes as if she were blind.) Cramer then taught a few brief lessons to help the kids understand how one teacher in one room could teach a group ranging in age from 5 to 14. They recited poetry together, took turns reading aloud from an original nineteenth-century reader, and stood in twos in front of the class to learn multiplication. She showed them her vintage lunch pail and talked about what kids brought for lunch. Then they learned a rousing hand-clap game and were dismissed, with permission granted to ring the school bell on the way out. They were having so much fun that they begged me to ring the school bell again, so they could come running into school in character. Just doing this was so thrilling that I had to ring the school bell six more times, for six more school entrances.

Not many historic sites would let kids ring school bells as often as they please, or run as freely as they wish, but the Sullivans, who own and operate the Homestead, don't want this to be a typical historic site. "When we bought this place a few years ago, we traveled around to the various Ingalls towns to see what they were doing," says Tim Sullivan. "No one was doing much of anything for families, and because we have four kids, we thought we'd take on the job."

It seemed clear to Erin and Emily that the people who run the Homestead understand children. They delighted at the rules posted in the main building/souvenir shop: "(1) Children Should Touch, Feel, and Climb; (2) Feel Free to Explore; and (3) Feel Free to Take Pictures of Everything." They didn't care that the tiny house Pa built was a replica and not the original—they were too busy pretending to cook on the iron stove and pretending to sew at Ma's prized sewing machine. They climbed in old covered wagons, raced through daisy-strewn prairie grass, rode a gentle horse, learned how to make rope, and, best of all, climbed up a ladder to the barn's hayloft, where they were overjoyed to discover a mama cat and her three kittens. The girls played with the kittens for ages, sharing them with the occasional kid who found his or her way up there. There was no guide to move them along, no show to see, no lecture to attend. Just a quiet afternoon on a prairie farm, where they were free to explore at will and lose themselves in a Little House fantasy.

The Itinerary

We have the increasing difficulty of family farming to thank for the Ingalls Homestead in De Smet. Tim and Joan Sullivan had been having a hard time making a success of their Iowa farm when they passed through De Smet and saw the old Ingalls property up for sale. They knew they could get some federal funding by restoring acreage to native prairie grass, and they saw an opportunity to combine tourism with a small amount of production farming to create a business that could include their four children. So they bought the place and set about making it a family attraction that would honor the spirit of the Laura Ingalls Wilder books.

Next, they began buying nineteenth-century buildings in the area and moving them to the Ingalls Homestead. There are two old white clapboard schoolhouses, one of which functions as a living-history schoolhouse, the other of which holds displays on covered-wagon travel, including an old wagon in excellent condition (and yes, kids can climb and touch and experience). There's an exact replica of the two-room house Pa built, complete with hay-stuffed mattresses, iron stove, kitchen gear, quilting rack, and a rocking chair like the one Pa made for Ma. There's a cramped, damp sod dugout, much like the one the Ingalls lived in on Plum Creek in Wisconsin. There's a big ol' barn with a hayloft and stalls for the horses that haul the wagons and give children rides. There's an old garage for repairing buggies, making rope, and doing other handy things. And there are a variety of covered wagons, from rickety old iron-wheeled ones to spiffy new rubber-wheeled ones used for rides. There's also, of course, a newer building to house the obligatory gift shop. Surrounding the buildings and wagons is the rest of the original homestead land, 100 acres of which were reseeded to prairie grasses in 1998, and 10 acres of which are farmed the way Pa farmed, with a horse-drawn plow. (Visitors on Memorial Day get to help plant the summer corn.)

Off in a corner of the property is the publicly owned Ingalls Memorial, where a plaque honoring the original site of the Ingallses' cabin is guarded by the five cottonwood trees that Pa planted at the end of *By the Shores of Silver Lake,* one each for Ma, Mary, Laura, Carrie, and Grace.

All this is set on a few acres of prairie, with miles of sky overhead and the sounds of birds everywhere. Children are encouraged to explore as they wish, so while some are having a "lesson" in the old schoolhouse, others can play house in the cabin or play tag out in the prairie grass.

A mile north of the Homestead is De Smet, a proud little county seat that calls itself "The Little Town on the Prairie." It's positively thick with Ingalls and Wilder connections. The nonprofit Laura Ingalls Wilder Memorial Society maintains and offers tours of the Surveyors House, where the family lived during their first De Smet winter, and the Ingalls Home, which Pa built in 1887 when he and Ma decided to move into town from the Homestead. Elsewhere around town you'll find the little schoolhouse the Ingalls girls attended (it's now a private home, marked with a plaque); the hardly changed main street, Calumet, which still has the Loftus Store, mentioned by Laura in the books; various streets named Ingalls and Wilder; the De Smet Depot Museum, full of prairie-life memorabilia; and the cemetery in which Pa, Ma, Mary, Carrie, and Grace are buried, along with other people who figure in the books. On the edge of town is an historical marker and view spot commemorating Silver Lake, which, sadly, was drained by local farmers decades ago for irrigation.

You can pass through De Smet (about an hour from the pretty town of Brookings and about two hours from Sioux Falls) for a few hours and just visit the Ingalls Homestead, but to get the most out of the experience, try to spend a night or two in the area. To really get into the mood, we'd recommend camping out, so you can see the stars the way Laura did; the best choices are Lake Thompson State Park (800-710-CAMP), on the shores of South Dakota's largest lake, just five miles south of De Smet, or the town's own Washington Park, a green city park that allows tent camping and has ten RV hookups (there are no reservations—you just pay on the honor system). The Ingalls Homestead also allows camping in some of its covered wagons and in a rustic bunkhouse. Those who prefer a well-made bed should stay at the Prairie House Manor, a family-friendly B&B that was built in 1894 by Banker Ruth, a minor character in the books.

If you have a full day, start with the guided tour offered by the Wilder Memorial Society. It only lasts about a half hour, and it will give you and your children some worthwhile background. After that, you can explore town a bit, checking out the various places to see and getting a bite to eat (our kids liked the Frosty Corner Café). Then plan on spending a whole afternoon at the Ingalls Homestead, allowing time for school, wagon rides, exploring, playing, and souvenir shopping.

Visitors in late June and July won't want to miss the annual Laura Ingalls Wilder Pageant, held on weekend evenings out on the prairie, with Pa's cottonwood trees in the background. It's a wonderful homespun amateur event put on by the folks in De Smet, with local kids playing the parts of Laura and her sisters.

MORE INGALLS HOMESTEADS

Much has been preserved or re-created of the various Ingalls and Wilder homes in the Midwest, and devout pilgrims visit every site. None are as hands-on as the Ingalls Homestead in De Smet, but each has its charms. Here are the highlights:

PEPIN, WISCONSIN • Near the handsome lakeside town of Pepin lies a replica of the log cabin in which the Ingalls family lived during Pa's fur-trapping days, when

Laura was very young—the *Little House in the Big Woods* era. ✂ The Little House Wayside, eight miles north of town on County Highway CC, (715) 442-3011

WALNUT GROVE, MINNESOTA • This is where the Ingalls family lived in *On the Banks of Plum Creek*. Plum Creek remains beautiful and unchanged, though the almost-empty town itself has seen better days. It does, however, have a decent little museum, rich in pioneer memorabilia if light on actual Ingalls artifacts. For three weeks in July, the town puts on a Laura Ingalls Wilder pageant. Twenty miles out of town is a pair of replica "soddies" set on ten acres of restored prairie. The "poor" sod house gives you a good idea of the miserable dugout in which the Ingalls family lived at Plum Creek; the "rich" soddie, finished with plaster and wood, is a cozy little B&B cabin. ✂ McCone Sod Houses, east of Walnut Grove on the Laura Ingalls Wilder Memorial Highway, (507) 723-5138; Laura Ingalls Wilder Museum, 330 8th Street, (507) 859-2358; pageant information (888) 859-3102

BURR OAK, IOWA • Wilder never wrote a novel about the year her family lived in this now-minuscule town, when she was 9 and the Ingallses had fallen on particularly hard times. They took a job running the Masters Hotel, which provided beds and food for the travelers passing through what was then a booming wagon crossroads—Pa ran the hotel, Ma cooked, and the three little girls (Grace wasn't born yet) cleaned and waitressed. It's a well-run tourist attraction run by local volunteers. ✂ Laura Ingalls Wilder Museum, Masters Hotel, Main Street, (563) 735-5916

MANSFIELD, MISSOURI • In 1894, Laura, Almanzo, and their young daughter, Rose, traveled by covered wagon to this farm town in the Ozarks and settled for good. Today Rocky Ridge Farm, with its handsome white farmhouse, stone house built by Rose, and museum filled with Ingalls and Wilder family memorabilia, is a booming tourist destination. Many a middle-aged woman who loved the Little House books as a girl has become weepy at the sight of Pa's burnished old fiddle. Also on display is the desk at which Wilder wrote all nine books. ✄ Laura Ingalls Wilder Home and Museum, Route 1, (417) 924-3626 or (877) 924-7126

NEWBERY GIRLS IN WISCONSIN

Two other titles about girls in the rural Midwest have important places in children's literature libraries. ✄ When Carol Ryrie Brink wrote *Caddie Woodlawn* in 1935, her grandmother, Caddie Woodlawn, was 82 and still as handy with hammer and nails as with a needle and thread. Based on her grandmother's stories of a pioneer childhood, this Newbery Award–winning novel is full of the spirit and "wildness" of young Caddie and her brothers, with dramatic incidents ranging from prairie fire to falling through the ice into the river. As tensions between white settlers and Native Americans ignite, Caddie makes a midnight ride to warn her Indian friends of an impending attack. You can visit the childhood home of Caddie Woodlawn in Menomonie, Wisconsin. ✄ Another Wisconsin farm girl is 9-year-old Garnet Linden, heroine of the 1939 Newbery-winning novel *Thimble Summer* by Elizabeth Enright. A charming, humorous story based on the author's midwestern farm childhood, this book for 9- to 12-year-olds is about a girl's eventful summer that begins with finding a "magic" thimble and culminates in winning a blue ribbon with her pig at the fair. Kids like it because Garnet, unlike so many contemporary heroines of books for this age group, is depicted at a happy time of her life. That's the point.

Names and Numbers

Ingalls Homestead
Homestead Rd., 1 mile
    southeast of De Smet
(800) 776-3594
Open Memorial Day–Labor
Day daily 9:30 A.M.–7 P.M.
Open during school year for
groups and field trips by
appointment.

Laura Ingalls Wilder
    Memorial Society
105 Olivet Ave.
De Smet
(800) 880-3383
www.liwms.com
Open daily for tours June–
Sept.; Mon.–Sat. Oct.,
Apr., and May; Mon.–Fri.
Nov.–Mar.

Laura Ingalls Wilder Pageant
(605) 692-2108
Performances held late
June–mid-July, 9 P.M.

Prairie House Manor Bed
    and Breakfast
Third St. and Poinsett Ave.
De Smet
(800) 297-2416
www.bbonline.com/sd/prairie/

The Little Red Lighthouse and the Great Gray Bridge (1942)

BY HILDEGARDE H. SWIFT AND LYND WARD

New York City

The little red light-house lives in a part of New York that's almost never seen by tourists: on the banks of the Hudson River near Washington Heights, in the shadow of the George Washington Bridge. The easy way to see the lighthouse is to take the Circle Line boat tour but don't discount the value of taking the subway up to 181st Street, to spend time right next to the lighthouse in beautifully situated but little-known Fort Washington Park. —CDB

This trip is ideal for families with readers between the ages of 4 and 8, but older children who love the book will also have fun.

The Book

Here's a quick test to spot native New Yorkers—ask if they know of this book, and see if they immediately light up. What

Make Way for Ducklings is for native Bostonians, *The Little Red Lighthouse and the Great Gray Bridge* is for native New Yorkers: a fixture of both their childhood literary landscape and everyday landscape. Tourists don't often see the real Jeffrey's Hook Lighthouse, because it is located far uptown, under the George Washington Bridge, but locals pass it often, as they drive along Henry Hudson Parkway or Riverside Drive on the Manhattan side, or along Henry Hudson Drive or Palisades Interstate Parkway on the New Jersey side.

But the lighthouse and the book mean much more to New Yorkers than just honoring a quaint landmark. For six decades, they have symbolized a child's life in New York. Both the lighthouse itself and its fictionalized story convey what it's like to be a very, very small part of a giant city—and how even the very, very small can make important contributions and be brave, valued, and loved. So cherished was this book that, nine years after its publication, it inspired the children of New York to help save the lighthouse from being sold and moved.

Swift's tale about Jeffrey's Hook Lighthouse (built in 1880 and moved to its current site in 1921) describes how important the lighthouse was in its early days as it guided ships along the Hudson. As the story develops, the proud little lighthouse becomes alarmed and confused by the construction that begins around him. Over time, he sees the giant bridge built. Then one night, he sees a huge, powerful light sweeping back and forth from high atop the bridge. That very same night, for the first time ever, the man who turns on the lighthouse's lantern doesn't come.

> *Now I am needed no longer . . .*
> *Perhaps they will give me up.*
> *Perhaps they will tear me down.*

Later that night, a thick fog blankets the river, and disaster looms. The great gray bridge calls to the lighthouse, wondering why his light isn't shining. When the lighthouse answers that he thought he was no longer needed, the bridge replies, "I call to the airplanes. . . . You are still master of the river. . . . Each to his own place, little brother!"

But the lighthouse can't turn on his own light, and the man still hasn't come. Convinced that he will never shine again, the lighthouse grows very sad. Then the man comes rushing in, explaining that ne'er-do-well boys had stolen his keys. He promises to never leave the lighthouse untended again.

Beside the towering gray bridge the lighthouse still bravely stands. Though it knows now that it is little, it is still VERY, VERY PROUD.

Little is brave, little is needed, little is even powerful. What child doesn't appreciate that message? They also appreciate the relationship of the man to the lighthouse—almost all kids have had parents arrive late to pick them up from school or day care at least once. They know the feeling of worry and possible abandonment, followed by the happy relief of a reunion and a restoration of order.

In reality, several years after the book was published, the little red lighthouse became less needed, and the Coast Guard finally shut it down in 1948. Three years later, it was put up for sale. The children of New York were outraged. One 4-year-old boy offered to buy it himself to keep it under the bridge. Kids and parents wrote angry letters. Newspapers published editorials condemning the sale. A prominent child psychologist said the lighthouse was a symbol of security for children, proving that "even though you are little in a big world, you won't be annihilated." The hue and cry finally inspired New

York's commissioner of parks to get the Coast Guard to donate the lighthouse to the city, and it became part of Fort Washington Park.

The Experience

Oh, sure, we could have taken the Circle Line for a leisurely cruise and seen the lighthouse from the deck. But it seemed like a greater adventure to find it on our own. So Emily and I boarded the A train in midtown and rode way, way uptown, past some pretty desolate subway stations, to 181st Street.

Usually my sense of direction is infallible, but this time I led us astray, walking east instead of west, not realizing the mistake until we were almost to the East River. But we didn't mind—it was invigorating to be in the midst of a thriving, multi-ethnic, working-class commercial district: food carts, street vendors hawking cheap watches and T-shirts, storefronts crammed with budget goods, and people everywhere.

Finally, we turned around and headed west on 181st toward the Hudson River. The shops gave way to apartments, and we found the footbridge that crossed the Hudson Parkway and led to a tree-shaded asphalt path winding gradually down the embankment toward the river. It was shabbier than Central Park, with more litter, but pretty nonetheless, with the Hudson sparkling in the sun. Since it was early spring and still quite cold, we had the park to ourselves, and after our long morning of walking, we sat down for a rest and a picnic at one of the tables near the little red lighthouse. The bridge soared overhead, so high up that we could barely hear the cars whizzing along it, and the lighthouse looked so wee and adorable in comparison that it seemed like a toy. Even though it was closed to the public, this being off-season, the little red lighthouse became a friend that day. A couple of boats chugged by, and we waved enthusiastically, in honor of the light that no longer shines but still burns inside every New York child who ever loved this book and this lighthouse.

TAR BEACH AND THE GREAT GRAY BRIDGE

Before setting out on any journey to see the little lighthouse and the looming George Washington Bridge, make sure to also read Faith Ringgold's Caldecott Honor book, *Tar Beach*. Based on a story quilt she made, this intensely colorful picture book is set in Washington Heights, on a blacktop roof (a "tar beach") where a little girl and her family go on hot summer nights. The great gray bridge is a key character—it is beloved by the girl because it signifies beauty and freedom to her, and because her father helped build it. This is a lovely book, eloquently conveying the yearning of a working-class city girl who dreams of flying over her city and making her father rich, so he'd never have to deal with racism and unemployment again.

The Itinerary

There are three ways to see the lighthouse. You can take the three-hour Circle Line cruise, a fancy red-and-white boat that circles the whole of Manhattan, with a guide describing the sights and history. If you have a car, you can drive past it on the Henry Hudson Parkway. Or you can get up close and personal, either by parking your car on or near 181st Street or by taking the subway there, then hoofing it down to Fort Washington Park.

The boat ride has its advantages, and kids usually love boat rides, but if your kids are under 8 (and this is a book most loved by the 3-to-6 crowd), a three-hour ride is likely to be two and a half hours too long. Driving by on a busy parkway doesn't make for much of an experience. So that leaves making the trek to Fort Washington Park as the ideal outing. To do it right, plan your visit for sometime between May and October, and call the Urban Park Rangers first to schedule a tour. It truly is a little lighthouse, so the tour doesn't take long, but it's well worth the effort—every kid loves going inside a real lighthouse.

Even better, try to come for the annual Little Red Lighthouse Festival, a low-key September event with family-friendly activities: lighthouse tours, hayrides, fair food, a celebrity reading of the book, and entertainment of the juggling/bluegrass variety. (Call the Urban Park Rangers for festival dates and details.)

One caveat: It's perhaps a half-mile or more walk from the subway station (or the street parking) to the park, and since it's downhill, even little kids can manage it fine. But it's uphill going back, and the whining could get serious with young ones. Consider bringing a stroller or wagon to help haul them back after your lighthouse fun.

Names and Numbers

Circle Line
Pier 83, W. 42nd St.
New York City
(212) 563-3200
Cruises daily Mar.–Nov.

Urban Park Rangers
(212) 304-2365

Fort Washington Park
Hudson River, from 155th St.
    north to Dyckman St.
New York City
(800) 201-PARK (NYC Parks
    and Recreation Dept.)

Little Women (1868)

BY LOUISA MAY ALCOTT

Concord, Massachusetts

*I*t looks like just another pretty village in Boston's orbit, but Concord played a huge part in American history, literature, and culture. The Revolutionary War kicked off here. Henry David Thoreau, Ralph Waldo Emerson, and Nathaniel Hawthorne lived, thought, and wrote here. And on a tiny desk in her family's home here, Louisa May Alcott wrote *Little Women,* one of the most loved stories ever produced by an American author. A day in Concord will not only please the *Little Women* fan in your family, but will hold appeal for history students, philosophers, and Revolutionary War buffs. —CDB

This trip is ideal for families with readers between the ages of 10 and 13.

The Book

It's understandable if the e-mail generation balks at reading about four sisters in Civil War times whose days were filled with such thrilling tasks as sewing, learning lessons, and tending to an elderly aunt. By today's standards, the writing is flowery, and the March sisters (and their mother, Marmee) are prone to such arch-sounding exclamations as "What fun it was!" They're also moralizing constantly ("Don't let's grumble, but shoulder our bundles and trudge along as cheerfully as Marmee does"). Can today's sometimes self-indulgent mall girls possibly be interested in such a book?

Apparently they can—*Little Women* earns a new army of 12-year-old fans every year. For even though the writing style is dated, and the girls at first seem hopelessly prim and prissy, the tales of their daily life quickly become absorbing. By the third chapter, you find yourself caring a great deal about whether Father will make it home safely from the Civil War, whether the mysterious boy next door will prove to be a good friend, and whether Jo will get that temper under control. (Although, truth be told, many girls don't take to the book at age 11 or 12, but discover it later as teenagers or, in my case, at 42.)

Louisa May Alcott based the book largely on her own life, which may be why it radiates such warmth and authenticity. Like the character Jo, Louisa was the second of four daughters, a born writer and tomboy with an independent streak. Meg, the oldest, prettiest, and most theatrically gifted, was based on the eldest sister, Anna; Amy, the youngest, shared the artistic talent of Louisa's youngest sister, May; and the wise, loving, hardworking Marmee was based on the wise, loving, hardworking Abigail May Alcott. (Although Louisa was very close to her well-known father, Bronson Alcott, his erratic life was too difficult for the young novelist to portray, so she sent his fictional counterpart, Mr. March, off to the war.)

Louisa insisted that each of the fictional sisters was based only in part on the actual sisters and that many of their character traits were invented; the exception was the third sister, Beth, the shy, sensitive musician, who was modeled exactly on Louisa's sister Beth. Sadly, there was one difference: In the book, Beth recovers from a terrible illness, but in real life she did not recover, and the entire Alcott family was left brokenhearted. So devasted was Louisa by her sister's death that she couldn't bring herself to write about Beth in *Little Women* until ten years later.

Most of *Little Women* takes place in the March family home, which is believed to have been modeled on Orchard House, the Alcott's Concord home from 1858 to 1877. When the book opens, the girls (ranging in age from 11 to 16) are preparing for their first Christmas without their father, who has gone off to war. They are in greatly reduced circumstances, Mr. March having "lost his property" while trying to help a friend, but are doing their best to be brave and plucky. This sets the stage for an entire book filled with bravery and pluckiness.

The eldest two must help support the family, Meg as a governess and Jo as a companion to an elderly, crotchety aunt. Beth is too shy for school and too young for work, so she helps at home, and Amy goes to school and tries to be useful. But their lives are not all drudgery. They have great fun putting on elaborate plays in the sitting room. They go ice-skating in winter and on picnics in summer. They cultivate a rewarding friendship with Laurie, the orphan boy who lives with his rich grandfather next door. They gather around Marmee for the weekly reading of Father's letter. They help each other navigate the wealthier social world outside their door, piecing together suitable gowns for balls, fixing each other's hair, and giving each other advice.

They are not perfect—the girls can get petulant and sometimes even selfish—but they try to be good daughters, sisters, and citizens, and their efforts manage to be both entertaining and captivating, even by today's standards. And there is drama. Will Amy survive her fall through the ice? Will Father make it home alive? Will Meg be shunned at the ball for having such a shabby dress? Will Laurie continue his studies and stay with his stern grandfather, or indulge his fantasies and run off to see the world? Will Beth pull through her terrible scarlet fever?

Will Meg fall in love with Mr. Brooke? Will Jo ever forgive Meg if she marries Mr. Brooke? *Little Women*'s millions of fans know the answers, and loved every moment of discovering— and rediscovering—them.

The Experience

There were seven of us—including mothers, daughters (ages 11, 12, and 13), and aunts—trooping into Orchard House on a cold March day, a group of big and little women on a pilgrimage. Some adored *Little Women*; others had enjoyed it well enough; and one had never read it at all. We all came away enchanted with Louisa May, her little women, her real-life family, and Concord life 130 years ago.

Each of us found our own particular source of delight that day. For some of us grown-ups, it was discovering that our own spiritual beliefs were shared by Bronson Alcott and that, unbeknownst to us, they were part of the movement called Transcendentalism, of which Alcott was a proponent in the nineteenth century. For 13-year-old Patti, it was seeing the actual costume trunk in May's (Amy's) room and the back staircase that the girls used to reach the "stage" for their plays. For grown-up Lynn, it was seeing Louisa's tiny writing desk, built for her by her father during a time when it was considered unladylike for women to have a desk. For 11-year-old CeCe, it was poring over the dollhouse dioramas of the March family at home. And for 12-year-old Megan, it was discovering that not only was young May (Amy) allowed to draw on the walls, but 130 years later, people were going to great trouble to preserve her wall art.

Some of the sociohistorical context we were given during the tour was fascinating to the adults and uninteresting to the kids. But some of it resonated with them. They were amazed to hear that Bronson Alcott was considered a radical educator for believing that girls should be able to attend school just like boys and that music and art should be part of an education. They understood that his beliefs, along with Abigail Alcott's independent streak (she was one of the first paid social workers in Massachusetts), helped give Louisa the foundation and inspiration to write about young girls as they really were, not as society expected them to be. This, our girls learned, had never been done before.

Having been raised on stories of the South's slavery but relatively unaware of the North's racism, the girls in our group were also amazed to hear that Mr. Alcott's theretofore successful private school in Boston went out of business when he admitted a black girl (the rest of the wealthy families fled in protest). And they got a kick out of hearing about how Louisa was hounded by fans, just like Britney Spears is today—once *Little Women* became a best-seller, devotees stood outside Orchard House every day, hoping to catch a glimpse of Louisa in her room upstairs, writing at her little desk. To get some peace, she finally started sneaking off to a Boston hotel room to write.

The two littlest women in our group came away from Orchard House inspired to start keeping journals, the way Jo/Louisa did. "Maybe I'll be a famous writer someday," said Megan. "And people will make my house into a museum!"

PLAN AHEAD FOR PROGRAMS

Orchard House sponsors frequent programs for children, and it's well worth your trouble to plan a trip around one of these. They range from a one-hour living-history tour, with costumed staff in character, to a weeklong summer drama workshop, in which children act out scenes from Alcott's stories and write and perform their own skit. The most ambitious programs take place in summer, but every month finds something happening: journal-writing workshops, a February Valentine party with a Louisa May character, a hands-on exploration of Victorian times (and toys) for little kids, and more. Most require reservations; call or go to the Web site for details.

The Itinerary

Storybook Travels, you'll note, is light on authors' houses—they typically bore kids more quickly than a *Masterpiece Theatre* marathon. But any girl (and the rare boy) who loved *Little Women* will love visiting Orchard House, home of the Alcott family when Louisa wrote her masterpiece.

After passing through the perfect town of Concord, where the white picket fences gleam and the Colonial saltboxes look as if they're repainted every morning, you'll probably do a double-take at the relative shabbiness of Orchard House, a big ol' brown-sided box. But that's exactly the way it should be— after all, the Alcott family was going through hard times, and they had to make do with a less elegant house (and less elegant clothing and trappings) than others in their social set.

All visitors to Orchard House, except those content to go no further than the gift shop, must take the guided tour. Before the tour, your small group will be shown into a room that once served as May's art studio. Some of her work adorns the walls, and across one end of the room is a dollhouse-style diorama of the various rooms in the Marches' house (modeled, of course, on Orchard House), with tiny dolls of the little women. You're given some time to poke around and look at the various items, one of which, curiously, is a circa-1999 TV and

VCR. The anachronism makes sense, however, when a docent pops in to turn on a video, which does a fine job of introducing Louisa May, her family, her work, and the house. A docent/actress portrays Louisa in middle age, reflecting on her work as a writer and describing how she wrote *Little Women,* what life was like with her family, and how her real family compared to the fictional March family. The video is absorbing, even for preteens.

Once the video ends, a docent takes you through the house. The good ones (and most are good) tailor their talks to the group, taking children's interests into account and playing up the tales of the girls' daily life. Unlike so many historic houses, this one is filled with the Alcotts' actual stuff, which makes it immediately more interesting to kids. Any old costume trunk is one thing, but when it's the actual one that the Alcott (March) sisters used to store their costumes in, well, that's pretty cool.

You progress through the bedrooms, kitchen, dining room, parlor, and study, hearing lots of stories en route. In Mr. and Mrs. Alcott's room is the dress that Anna (Meg) got married in, and you're likely to hear a story or two about family weddings. In Louisa's room is her tiny desk, many of her books, and paintings by her sister May. In May's room are wonderful wall drawings and paintings, the costume trunk, and the back stairs down to the dining room, which the young actresses ran up and down for costume changes during plays. In the kitchen is the fancy (by 1870 standards) sink Louisa bought her mother when *Little Women* became a hit. In the parlor is furniture on which Thoreau and Emerson sat when they came calling on Monday nights, when the Alcotts always had open house and the girls often put on plays. In the study are Bronson Alcott's desk and personal items, along with an extraordinary (and extraordinarily scandalous for its time) portrait of a black woman painted by May.

You end, of course, in the gift shop, which is low-key and full of crafts; the girls in our group snapped up spool-doll kits, paper-doll books, and the video of the 1994 film adaptation (quite a good one), written by Robin Swicord and starring Susan Sarandon as Marmee.

While Orchard House will be the heart and soul of any *Little Women* outing (allow about two hours for it altogether), you can spend a little more time exploring beyond its walls. Next door is The Wayside, where the Alcotts lived for three years when Louisa was a young teenager. (Nathaniel Hawthorne's family bought the house after the Alcotts; later it was bought and preserved by Margaret Sidney, author of *The Five Little Peppers and How They Grew.*) Now part of Minute Man National Historic Park, The Wayside doesn't have any Alcott artifacts, but many kids enjoy a quick visit to see the barn, where the sisters put on rousing plays.

Finally, you can take the fresh air the way the March sisters did—but with a whole lot less clothing (parasols optional)—by having a leisurely picnic at Walden Pond State Reservation, the park that encompasses the famed woods and pond that were once home to Louisa's tutor, Henry David Thoreau. Or if you're feeling more energetic, rent a canoe at South Bridge Boat House and try your hand at rowing on the Concord River, boating being another favorite *Little Women* outing.

HENRY HIKES TO FITCHBURG

If your group includes children too young to read *Little Women*, make sure to pick up the younger-kid storybook *Henry Hikes to Fitchburg*, by Donald B. Johnson. As a matter of fact, read the book even if your group doesn't include any little kids. It's a delightful tale about two bears who decide to visit Fitchburg, which is in the country north of their Concord home; one works and saves money for a train ride, while the other bear, Henry, who's been inspired by Henry David Thoreau, walks the 30 miles, collecting berries and flowers en route. It's a clever twist on the fable of the tortoise and the hare, and its simple introductions to Thoreau, the Alcotts, Emerson, and Hawthorne make it a fine companion for a Concord visit.

Names and Numbers

Orchard House
399 Lexington Road
Concord
(978) 369-4118
www.louisamayalcott.org
Open Apr.–Oct. Mon.–Sat.
10 A.M.–4:30 P.M., Sun.
1 P.M.–4:30 P.M.; Nov.–Mar.
Mon.–Fri. 11 A.M.–3 P.M.,
Sat. 10 A.M.–4:30 P.M.,
Sun. 1 P.M.–4:30 P.M.; closed
first two weeks of Jan.,
Easter, Thanksgiving, and
Christmas.

The Wayside
455 Lexington Road
Concord
(978) 369-6975
Open May–Oct.; call for
hours and tour times.

Concord Chamber of
   Commerce
2 Lexington Road
Concord
(978) 369-3120
www.concordmachamber.org

Concord History and
   Information
www.concordma.com

Walden Pond State
   Reservation
915 Walden St.
Concord
(978) 369-3254
www.state.ma.us/dem/parks/
   wldn.htm
Parking lot closes if number
of park visitors reaches
1,000.

South Bridge Boat House
496–502 Main St.
Concord
(978) 369-9438

Madeline (1939) & Other Titles

BY LUDWIG BEMELMANS

Paris, France

No one needs an excuse to visit Paris—except families, who often fear that the city's formal (some say haughty) urbanity makes it inhospitable to children. But with Madeline as their guide, children will be as enchanted by Paris as their adult companions. You can spend a whole day walking in Madeline's *chaussures* (shoes), or spread the outings over a few days, interspersed with other adventures.　　—CDB

This trip is ideal for families with readers between the ages of 5 and 10.

The Books

In an old house in Paris that was covered with vines
Lived twelve little girls in two straight lines. . . .

Few books (whether for children or adults) begin in a more evocative, romantic, and utterly charming manner. When *Madeline* became an immediate hit upon its publication in 1939, those opening lines were promptly memorized by thousands of children. Today their grandchildren and great-grandchildren can also recite from memory:

> *In two straight lines they broke their bread*
> *and brushed their teeth*
> *and went to bed.*
> *They smiled at the good*
> *and frowned at the bad*
> *and sometimes they were very sad.*

Overseen by a loving but stern nun, the girls sleep in plain iron beds, wear starched blue uniforms, and march in line through the streets of Paris. In fact, French girls in the convent schools of sixty years ago led lives of such order and discipline that the success of the several Madeline books with today's American children seems mystifying.

Of course, there's more to young Madeline, the smallest of them all, than Gallic propriety and convent-school structure. Like all good literary heroines, she's brave and plucky, ready to take a risk and frighten Miss Clavel when the time seems right. Sometimes a bridge railing begs to be walked on, or a tiger at the zoo demands a challenge, or a Gypsy family includes a lost little girl in their travels. But while Madeline is a risk taker, she always returns to the comfort of Miss Clavel and her eleven hair-bow-adorned companions. This embodies the challenge of growing up for children—to experience new places, take risks, and have adventures, always with the reassurance that the adults in charge will guide them safely. And at journey's end, they know they'll return to their own beds and the routine of regular life.

Of the several Madeline books, two are required reading for any visitor to Paris: the original, *Madeline,* and the first sequel, *Madeline's Rescue.* In the first, we meet the little girls, Miss Clavel, and the old house covered with vines. We get to know the girls as they skitter about Paris like rows of uniformed sandpipers: across the Place Vendôme, past the Eiffel Tower, and Notre Dame, in front of the Basilique du Sacré-Coeur. Most of the great Parisian landmarks are sketched out in that first book, although the two central locations, the school and the hospital where Madeline's appendix is removed, are fictional.

In *Madeline's Rescue,* Madeline's daring goes a bit too far, and she falls into the Seine. A clever dog saves her from a watery grave, and the dog returns to the old house to live with the girls. Christened Genevieve, she becomes a beloved member of the household until the dreaded day of the annual trustees' inspection. Genevieve is discovered under a bed and banished by prissy Lord Cucuface, who feels that a mutt has no place with proper young ladies. The dog departs, the girls wail, and Madeline declares war on Cucuface. Although the war never happens, Madeline doesn't give up hope that Genevieve will be found, and sure enough, she returns, promptly giving birth to an even dozen puppies, who soon join the girls on their daily walks through Paris.

The Experience

We arrived in Paris the night before, after an eleven-hour drive with two homesick children who'd been traveling for nearly six weeks. In the morning the kids had their first Parisian hotel breakfast, featuring flawless little croissants and steaming hot chocolate. While they ate, my husband and I could almost see the little thought balloons over their heads: "Maybe this big, crowded city won't be so bad after all."

Two Métro rides later, we approached the Seine. Boats plowed the water, pigeons strolled the quay, and Notre Dame stood watch over it all. We set off across Pont Neuf, neither child thrilling to the surroundings the way we Paris-mad parents were. Mostly they were consumed by fear of lunchtime, having been tipped off by their more sophisticated friends that Parisians routinely eat such disgusting things as snails and eels.

Midway across, 5-year-old Emily came to a dead stop. "This is the bridge where Madeline fell off!" she shrieked. And indeed it was . . . as far as we can tell from Bemelmans's airy, freewheeling sketches. (It may also have been Pont Royal, just off the Quay Voltaire, because Bemelmans made his first sketches for *Madeline* while sitting at a sidewalk table at the now-defunct Restaurant Voltaire, on the quay.)

Until that revelatory moment, Paris had seemed overwhelming to Emily. But after connecting with Madeline's Paris, she began to see it on her scale. Her homesickness receded and her excitement bubbled over; suddenly she was ready to explore the city she'd known only from a picture book. Even her more cynical older sister, Erin, who'd always thought that Madeline was a little dopey, got caught up in the spirit. We put the food fears to rest by refueling with the ubiquitous *steak haché et frites* (hamburger and fries), then set off in search of an old house covered with vines.

Part of Paris's profound attraction for adults is the opportunity to be in the same cafés, on the same streets, and in the same buildings as many of the greatest writers, artists, and musicians of the last two centuries. If a child loves the *Madeline* books, he or she will experience essentially the same attraction.

MADELINE ON FILM AND DISK

Before a Europe trip, consider getting *Madeline's Europe,* a CD-ROM produced by Creative Wonders. Aimed at ages 4–8, it follows Madeline on a quest for her missing friend Genie. As kids join her in the search, they'll learn about several European cities and pick up some French and Spanish words. ✖ Also well worth a video rental is the feature film *Madeline,* starring Frances McDormand as Miss Clavel. While not entirely successful, it does capture the spirit of the book, and much of it was filmed on location in central Paris. It was released shortly after we went to Paris, and our kids adored revisiting the places they'd just been to.

The Itinerary

The logical place to begin an exploration of Madeline's Paris is a quest for the old house covered with vines. Begin with a Métro ride to the Courcelles stop in the Eighth Arrondissement and set off on foot along the rue de Courcelles toward avenue Hoche; the Parc Monceau will be on your left. Adults will love the neighborhood's fine eighteenth- and nineteenth-century homes, over which crawl vines that bloom spectacularly in summer. This was Proust's neighborhood (45, rue de Courcelles), and he'd still feel at home here. (Tell the kids that a writer named Proust who lived in this neighborhood became very famous for writing a story about eating madeleines. It's a delicious coincidence.)

Poke around the park neighborhood, walking down little streets like avenue Van-Dyck and rue Murillo, and have a contest: Which house looks most like Madeline's? It's a great way to help your child fall in love with Parisian neighborhoods. (And if you hear young American voices, don't be surprised—a French-American school is nearby.)

Once you've picked your old vine-covered house, do what Madeline would have done and march through Parc Monceau until you find one of the playgrounds. It's a lovely park, a great place for a romp and perhaps a picnic.

If you come out the east end of the park, by the corner of boulevard Malesherbes and boulevard de Courcelles, you'll see Montmartre looming not far away. It's one of the landmark neighborhoods that pops up in both *Madeline* books. If you all have energy, walk up there and explore.

From here on out, you can visit as many Bemelmans-illustrated Parisian sites as you can manage. The most essential is, of course, a walk across a bridge near Notre Dame, which the twelve girls are often pictured doing, and from which Madeline fell in *Madeline's Rescue*. Notice the way the Seine flows in the book; now that you're on the bridge, you'll see that it flows the opposite way, a fact that much embarrassed Bemelmans later when he realized his mistake.

Another essential kid stop is the Eiffel Tower—though it never plays a part in a Madeline adventure, it's featured in many of the illustrations. Emily knew the Eiffel Tower from these books alone and couldn't wait until she went up it herself. Accept that it will be mobbed and overpriced and that the wait will be tedious. First-time visitors, especially children, don't mind a bit and will find all the bother to be eminently worthwhile. Bring along a paperback copy of one of the books to read in line—it will probably attract other kids, and it will help your child learn how to make herself comfortable during a long wait.

Elsewhere, use the books as your inspiration. Head to Place

Vendôme and watch for bad guys, like the purse snatcher who makes the girls "frown at the bad." If it rains, take umbrellas and walk to Notre Dame like the girls did. When exploring St-Germain-des-Prés, stop for a soda at Les Deux Magots, the café made famous by Hemingway and his peers. In *Madeline's Rescue,* the girls tip over the sidewalk tables looking for Genevieve; you're sure to see at least one pampered pooch sitting under a table—or on a lap. The girls also look for their dog at the famous Père Lachaise cemetery, as well as in the Tuileries, one of the French parks in which American kids can see evidence that dogs can seem more welcome in Paris than children. If you visit between June 21 and August 25, the Tuileries will be hosting its annual carnival with a great Ferris wheel; read *Madeline and the Gypsies* before attending the carnival.

Many American children mistakenly think that Madeline is an orphan, so don't forget to explain that the "old house" was a convent school, not an orphanage. Well-bred young ladies of that era were sent off to convent schools to be schooled and mannered; they saw their families only on school holidays. Ludwig Bemelmans's mother went to such a school.

To help your children get in the spirit of living like proper young Parisian ladies and gentlemen, consider taking them shopping for appropriate new outfits. Once they're scrubbed, brushed, and shipshape, take them to Angélina, a dress-up, Belle Epoque tearoom that serves the most decadent hot chocolate imaginable. Madeline never visits Angélina in her books, but surely her papa took her there on school holidays.

> *"Good night little girls!*
> *Thank the Lord you are well!*
> *And now go to sleep!"*
> *said Miss Clavel.*

Names and Numbers

French Government Tourist
    Office
444 Madison Ave.
New York City
(212) 838-7800
www.francetourism.com

Paris Tourism Office
127 ave. des Champs-
    Elysées, 8th Arr.
Paris
(33-1) 49-52-53-54
English-language events
hot line, (33-1) 49-52-53-56
Open daily 9 A.M.–8 P.M.

Angélina
226 rue de Rivoli, 1st Arr.
Paris
(33-1) 42-60-82-00
Closed Tues. in Aug.

Les Deux Magots
6 pl. St-Germain-des-Prés,
    6th Arr.
Paris
(33-1) 45-48-55-25
Open daily.

Make Way for Ducklings (1941)

BY ROBERT MCCLOSKEY

Boston, Massachusetts

A compact, handsome city, Boston has a friendly American urbanity that makes it very accessible for visiting families. The Mallard family's Boston is also the heart of tourist Boston, so walking the ducks' walk will also serve as a perfect small-scale introduction to the city for children who are too young to know (or care) about Paul Revere and tea-dumping revolutions.

—CDB

This trip is ideal for families with readers between the ages of 4 and 7.

The Book

The enduring appeal of certain simple picture books often seems a mystery. Such is the case for *Make Way for Ducklings.* It has the elements common in countless storybooks, most of which vanish into obscurity after a few years: baby animals, a journey, a friendly policeman, a reunion with a parent, and just a wee bit of danger. Somehow Robert McCloskey managed to combine these universal ingredients into a classic book that delights today's 4-year-olds while bringing nostalgic joy to 45-year-olds, many of whom take pride in being able to remember and recite the names of all eight ducklings (in case you've forgotten, they are Jack, Kack, Lack, Mack, Nack, Ouack, Pack, and Quack).

A no-frills narrative and McCloskey's exuberant, large-scale charcoal drawings tell the story of Mr. and Mrs. Mallard, who are searching Boston for a place to hatch their babies. They become smitten with the Public Garden, but then a close encounter with a kid on a bike sends them on a quest for a safer haven. They settle on a reedy little island in the Charles River, molt, make their nest, and swim across the river every day to visit Michael, a policeman who gives them peanuts. Finally, Mrs. Mallard lays her eggs, and soon there are eight ducklings.

As the baby ducks grow stronger, Mr. Mallard sets off to explore the Charles River, and the family agrees to reunite in the Public Garden in a week. Mrs. Mallard teaches the babies to swim, dive, walk in a line, and avoid bikes and other park dangers. Satisfied with their skills, she leads them across the river and into Boston. But the journey quickly becomes perilous as they encounter the big scary highway full of speeding, honking cars. Mrs. Mallard and her brood make such a quacking ruckus that Michael the policeman comes to the rescue, stopping traffic, escorting the ducks across the highway, and alerting fellow policemen to stop traffic on busy Beacon Street. The duck family proudly marches through Beacon Hill, past the Charles Street shops, and into the Public Garden, where they find Mr. Mallard waiting for them in the Swan Pond, as promised. The journey is successful, the family is reunited, and the ducklings are sure to have a long and happy life in this serene pond, living on peanuts and bread tossed by Boston's children.

The Experience

It was a cold and blustery day—not one that evoked frolicking ducklings, but the one that happened to find us in Boston. Undeterred, we battened down the hatches (gloves, hats, scarves) and set off to walk the walk. It took a little wandering to get our exact bearings—the highway has been fenced off for many years now and must be crossed via the Arthur Fiedler Bridge—but soon we were standing on the banks of the Charles, looking at the skinny little island where Mrs. Mallard hatched her eggs. "It doesn't look like a very good place to make baby ducks," said my 5-year-old nephew Will, who went on to wonder why there were no ducks on the river. I stumbled for a typically vague adult answer ("Maybe it's just too cold"), and off we set on the journey to the Public Garden.

Instead of the kindly Irish policeman, we had an impersonal but pleasantly twisty footbridge to get us across the highway. Instead of the Corner Book Shop, we saw the world's most discreet 7-Eleven on the corner of Charles and Mt. Vernon. But we felt just as happy and proud as that duck family as we marched through the red-brick beauty of Beacon Hill, Boston's posh old money neighborhood.

We got across Beacon Street with the help of a red light instead of policemen, entered the garden's gates, and soon found the bronze sculpture of Mrs. Mallard and her little ones. This necessitated a stop, of course, to pet and name each duckling and climb on Mrs. Mallard's back. Finally, we reached the ice-rimmed Swan Pond, where Will and his cousins shrieked with joy at finding ducks—lots and lots of ducks. "You're wrong—it's not too cold for ducks!" he hollered while hurling a piece of bread into the duck party. And I was happy to have been wrong.

ROBERT MCCLOSKEY AND NEW ENGLAND

In the '40s and '50s, Robert McCloskey turned out one fabulous New England–based children's book after another. Besides celebrating Boston in *Make Way for Ducklings*, he brings New England summertime berry-picking to life in *Blueberries for Sal*; has a slightly older Sal enjoy a perfect day with her family in *One Morning in Maine*; and uses glorious watercolors and lyrical writing to celebrate Maine in his most beautiful book, *Time of Wonder*. Read them all before any New England outing.

The Itinerary

This is a simple but rewarding outing that takes a couple of hours at a typical kindergartener speed (i.e., allowing for dawdling and detours). Start at the Arthur Fiedler Bridge, a curvy, concrete pedestrian bridge over the busy highway that so terrified the Mallard family. You'll pass the Hatch Shell (home of the Boston Pops) and will easily spot the island on which the ducks nested—it looks exactly as it does in the book, with the Longfellow Bridge in the background. This is a fine place to run and romp a bit; if the kids have scooters, they can cruise some of the famed Charles River bike path.

Then it's time to become the Mallard family and head off on the journey to meet Mr. Mallard. In a line, just like a proper duck family, head back across the Fiedler Bridge. Turn left when you leave the bridge and walk a block or so along the street that parallels the highway. Turn right on Mt. Vernon, a quiet residential street lined with red-brick houses that evoke the nineteenth century. You'll quickly find Charles Street, though you won't find the Corner Book Shop, which is long gone. Turn right on Charles Street and march past the fetching little boutiques and cafés, stopping for ice cream or hot chocolate if your ducklings are getting peckish.

After about two blocks, Charles opens onto busy Beacon Street. Again, instead of whistling policemen, you'll have to rely on crosswalks. Once across, enter the Public Garden gates on the right (the park space on the left is Boston Common), and you'll see Mrs. Mallard and her little ones in bronze, just waiting for a photo opportunity and some playtime. When it's time to move on, follow the park paths to the large Swan Pond. Here you'll find things just as they are depicted in the book: the little island on which the Mallard family lived; the bridge from which people toss peanuts and bits of bread to the many ducks (and, in season, the geese); and every child's favorite, the Swan Boats, which have been plying the pond for more than 120 years. (Take note that the boats disappear during the icy season, from about November until April.) These whimsical flat-bottomed boats cruise the pond for fifteen minutes, a perfect little-kid adventure. Make sure to bring some treats to toss to the ducks that will follow your boat around.

That's the extent of the ducklings' tour. If you still have energy, head off to explore the rest of the Public Garden and Boston Common, where you'll find a couple of good playgrounds and, over on the Common side, good ice-skating on quaint little Frog Pond.

The ducks slept happily on their little island in Swan Pond, but people aren't allowed on it. If you can afford it, consider sleeping at the Ritz-Carlton, which is known for its children's events, its location just across Arlington Street from the Swan Pond, and its general poshness. It hosts regular teddy-bear teas, kids' cooking classes, "social savvy" lessons for 8- to 12-year-olds, and Easter and Christmas kids' events, and its accommodations include the junior presidential suite: a colorful kids' room (stocked with bunk beds, toys, games, snacks, and videos), and an adjacent parents' room.

BOSTON AND BASEBALL

Well worth reading before or during a Boston visit is Matt Tavares's *Zachary's Ball* (2000), a lovely picture book whose story is reminiscent of *The Giving Tree*. It's set largely in Fenway Park, is richly illustrated, and is ideal for young baseball lovers. Try to schedule a baseball game around the reading of this book.

Names and Numbers

Boston Convention and
    Visitor's Bureau
2 Copley Pl., Ste. 105
Boston
(888) SEE-BOSTON
www.bostonusa.com

Swan Boats
Boston Public Garden
Beacon St. at Arlington St.
(617) 522-1966
Open April–Oct. or Nov.,
depending on weather.

The Ritz-Carlton Boston
15 Arlington St.
Boston
(617) 536-5700
(800) 241-3333

Maybelle the Cable Car (1952)

by Virginia Lee Burton

San Francisco, California

O f all the world's great urban icons, from the Eiffel Tower to the Empire State Building, none is more enticing to children than the San Francisco cable car, the subject of this sweet, idealistic storybook. Therefore the cable car—and this storybook—make fine focal points for a child's visit to San Francisco, which is quite possibly the world's best city for kid-friendly travel. Full of urban energy and high-rise dynamism, yet compact enough to not be overwhelming, it is packed with things children adore, from ferry boats to chocolate bars, soaring bridges to, yes, cable cars. —CDB

This trip is ideal for families with readers between the ages of 5 and 9.

The Book

Maybelle was a cable car
a San Francisco cable car
Cling clang . . . clingety clang
Up and down and around she went.

So begins the tale of the little cable car that could. Told in off-and-on rhyme by Virginia Lee Burton (who also wrote *Mike*

Mulligan and His Steam Shovel), the book starts with a simple description of Maybelle: her bell, her cable grip, her brakes, her conductor, and her gripman. She's a plucky little green-and-yellow gal, toting happy folks up and down the city's steepest streets, clanging all the way.

But trouble looms for Maybelle and her sisters. As their little city had grown large in the early decades of the twentieth century, the aging cable cars had been allowed to grow shabby. Along comes Big Bill, a pushy, exhaust-spewing bus who impresses the city fathers with his speed, capacity, and, most of all, profitability. Maybelle feels sad and unloved, worried about her future.

Ah, but Big Bill and the city fathers had underestimated San Franciscans' love for the rickety old cable cars! Midway through, the book recounts (in storybook fashion) the true tale of how the Citizens' Committee to Save the Cable Cars was formed, and how the residents of San Francisco, led by one woman as plucky as Maybelle, used petitions and the ballot box to save the old cars. (Burton doesn't give all the historical details, which would bore the kids, but just so you know, the woman was Friedel Klussman, and the year was 1947.) After a close call on a rainy day, Big Bill comes to realize that heavy buses can't handle the steep, slippery hills like cable cars can, and he and Maybelle become friends.

Maybelle's story ends up being as much about the political process as about cable cars. Through its simple story, cheerful watercolor illustrations, and can-do spirit, the book shows how a community can band together and protect the things they value. For children learning about endangered species, the story will resonate: fifty years ago, Maybelle was an endangered species of sorts, but today she and her kin are San Francisco's most cherished assets.

The Experience

When we first visited San Francisco as kids, in the '60s, a ride on a cable car was the most urgent item on the agenda. As parents, we've returned with our own children, as well as nephews, nieces, and friends' kids, and the priorities never vary: "When can we ride the cable car?"

The Bates family has a little tradition of one-on-one trips at certain ages. It starts at 7, with a mother-daughter trip to San Francisco. During Erin's trip at this age, we discovered Maybelle's book, but not until after we'd ridden the cars and visited the Cable Car Museum. So three years later, when Emily's turn came along, we read the book (three times) to get ready.

The first part of *Maybelle*, before Burton gets into the campaign to save the cable car, serves as a good primer on the city. It explains that it is a bay city (with water on three sides), a port city, and a hilly city. It explains how the little city grew larger and very rich, then was decimated by the Great Fire, but soon was rebuilt. And it tells the story of the cable cars: how they were invented to navigate the steep, steep hills, using brakes that tightly grip cables running under the city streets.

After reading *Maybelle*, Emily's desire to ride a cable car grew to an obsession. Unfortunately, the weekend of our visit turned out to be the busiest of the year, with about a hundred major conventions in town. Every cable car that clanged up Powell Street was as stuffed as a Chinatown dumpling, and the line at the terminus stretched on without end. If we spent half the day in line, we wouldn't have time for all the other fun we'd scheduled. So we set off on some of our other adventures—but Emily was sad every time we saw an overfull car clang by, especially when the car was painted green and yellow. "Oh, there's Maybelle," she'd say wistfully.

Finally we got smart. On Sunday morning after breakfast, we agreed on a challenge: to walk all the way up Powell Street, from Union Square to the top of Nob Hill. A local had promised that our reward would be a cable-car ride, and that was motivation enough for Emily to undertake the arduous climb. We stopped at each cable-car stop, both to catch our breath and to see if we could catch a ride. But each car was fuller than the last.

Just when Emily's complaining was about to do us both in, we made it to the top. What an achievement! What a view! And there was one of Maybelle's sisters—with lots of empty seats!

We'd discovered the secret. Because the California Street line goes to neither Union Square nor Fisherman's Wharf, it is little used by tourists. So we jumped on and rode the car to the western terminus at Van Ness Avenue. The sparse crowd on the car was made up of locals, who were charmed by the enthusiasm of the young tourist. Every "clang" was thrilling, every stop an adventure. At the end, everyone but us got off; we headed right back up California Street, just happy to be riding. Then Emily spotted a little nail salon boasting $7 manicures, and since she'd been promised a city-girl manicure for this trip, we hopped off and went in for some purple nail polish. Now that's urban living!

"I would *definitely* have voted to save the cable cars, Mom," said Emily. "Wouldn't you?"

The Itinerary

First things first: Get yourselves a ride on a cable car. Unfortunately, that's not as easy as it was years ago. The tourism boom and the increased popularity of San Francisco as a convention city and vacation destination mean that the lines to board at both the Market Street and Fisherman's Wharf stations stretch forever. All day long, every square inch of floorboard and wooden seat is taken. Or is it?

After many, many trips to the city by the bay, we've discovered two ways to enjoy painless cable-car rides. The first is Susan's favorite, because her family are early risers. The cars start running shortly after 6 A.M., and that's when she and her kids jump on the Powell line from Union Square to climb Nob Hill—in an empty car. They transfer at California and ride the California line downhill to the Financial District, where they hop off for breakfast. The crowds are still minimal when they've finished breakfast, so then they might just ride on over to Fisherman's Wharf.

The second is Colleen's favorite, and it was described above. Because no one in her family rises with the sun, they ride the California line, which runs from the less-glamorous Financial District to even-less-glamorous Van Ness. The kids don't care where they're going; they're just thrilled to get a seat and a good view of the gripman.

Once the cable car has been properly ridden, it's time to head over to the Cable Car Museum. (If you can get on a cable car on the Mason Street line, there's a stop right in front of the museum.) Built in 1907 after the Great Fire, this red-brick building is more than a museum—it's the functioning hub of the city's cable-car system, and it sits right on top of the giant, noisy sheave (pulley) system that keeps the cables moving. Inside, you can go below ground level to see the cables stretching off in several directions under the city streets, waiting to be grabbed by a cable car. Very little children might find it too noisy and intense, but most kids love seeing the giant wheels turn, and they suddenly understand how the cars work and why the gripmen have to be so strong.

Throughout the museum is a collection of old cars, some dating back to the cable car's creation in 1873. The more fragile models are hands-off, but kids can climb aboard a few. A number of pictorial displays recount the system's history, which generally bores kids, but seek out the mural that tells the story of the 1947 campaign to replace the cable cars with buses—the same story told in *Maybelle*. And don't miss the bell, which kids can ring with annoying abandon.

At one visit, Erin was more fascinated with the ancient 25-cent photo-viewfinders than the cable-car machinations. They're stocked with old black-and-white photographs of San Francisco before and after the 1906 earthquake and fire. She was amazed at the devastation, and even more amazed at how the city rebuilt itself. The photos really bring home a history lesson that is mentioned only briefly in the book.

No trip to a kid-friendly museum is complete without a visit to the gift shop, and the one here is the perfect place to buy a small replica of a cable car. It's also the place we first discovered *Maybelle the Cable Car.*

Names and Numbers

San Francisco Visitors and
    Convention Bureau
201 3rd St., Ste. 900,
San Francisco
(415) 391-2000
www.sfvisitor.org

Cable Car Museum
1201 Mason St., Nob Hill,
San Francisco
(415) 474-1887
www.cablecarmuseum.com
Open daily 10 A.M.–5 P.M.
(till 6 P.M. Apr.–Sept.)
Admission free.

Cable car schedule and
route information
San Francisco MUNI
(415) 673-MUNI
www.sfmuni.com
*Cable car tickets are sold
individually, or you can get
an all-day pass, also good*
*on all MUNI buses and
trolleys. Also check out
www.sfcablecar.com for history,
schedule details, route maps,
and a cool interactive cable
car that shows kids how the
cable-and-grip system works.*

Paddle-to-the-Sea (1941)

BY HOLLING CLANCY HOLLING

Niagara Falls, Canada

Several generations of readers have imagined the journey undertaken by Paddle-to-the-Sea, a toy wooden canoe carved by a Native American boy who sends the little boat along the Great Lakes to the Atlantic Ocean. Late-elementary readers who follow the maps and detailed illustrations in this still-intriguing book will thrill to a visit to the Canadian side of the falls, where they can re-live some of the canoe's experiences.   —SLT

This trip is ideal for families with readers between the ages of 8 and 13, and their younger (5–7) siblings.

The Book

When UCLA's Armand Hammer Museum of Art exhibited highlights of four hundred years of illustrated children's books, the works of Holling C. Holling (1900–1973) were selected to represent the twentieth century alongside the works of Dr. Seuss and Beatrix Potter. Curator Cynthia Burlingham wrote that Holling's books "evince a nostalgia for preindustrialized America, with rich illustrations and texts focusing on the country's natural resources and on Native Americans' interactions with the environment."

A weighty recommendation indeed, but classic books stay in print for just one reason: People buy them. The watercolors illustrating the Caldecott Award–winning *Paddle-to-the-Sea* are wonderful, but what makes the book memorable is the clever combination of illustrations, two-page chapters, maps, captions with additional factoids, and a thoroughly satisfying structure. You get the best of encyclopedia browsing along with an exciting story.

The story is simple. A Native American boy has learned that the snowmelt around his home in the Canadian wilderness will make its way via rivers and the Great Lakes to the Atlantic Ocean. He carves a wooden canoe with a boy (like himself) in it, and a message carved on the bottom that reads "Please put me back into water. I am Paddle-to-the-Sea." The boy sets the canoe outside on a snowbank and returns each day, until one day he sees a brook forming, and the little canoe floating away on the rushing water. We, the readers, follow along on the little canoe's journey.

In some ways, *Paddle-to-the-Sea* is a precursor to today's popular, accessible nonfiction books for elementary-school kids that use humor, graphic surprises, and quirky facts to make learning about science or history fun. In a less frenetic way, *Paddle* offers self-contained spreads for each segment of the journey, so the reader can happily look at the picture, read the story, and let his or her eye move around to various other small pictures and captions. Each segment has a small, simple map showing where Paddle is right now, and the book's endpapers are a large map showing the entire journey.

For children whose homes are anywhere along the canoe's

path (which crosses a dozen American states and Canadian provinces), the pleasure is in finding familiar landmarks and gradually having one's view widen from the local to the regional. Readers who live outside the region will get a painless geography lesson. And travelers will find a congenial companion.

Paddle moves through many a Great Lakes environment: the open water of Lake Superior, the calm backwater of a marsh, a fish camp in the Apostle Islands. But the central image of the book—a small, sturdy toy canoe journeying through a big, watery world—will be forever alive in the mind of a child who visits the main landmarks on the Canadian side of Niagara Falls.

The Experience

Irene and I joined the damp throngs of visitors in the perpetual drizzle on the plaza at Table Rock, a lookout area right at the eastern edge of Horseshoe Falls. Moving to the railing so we were just a few feet from the falls, we stood mesmerized by the steady rush of the water, gorgeously green as it hurried up from our right, then gradually turning white as it slipped, thousands of gallons at a time, over the edge, crashing below into foam and the celebrated mist. As Holling describes the scene:

> *"Mother! Look! A little man! In a boat!" a child screamed.*
> *She stood with the usual crowd of people . . . in the beautiful*
> *Canadian park overlooking the falls. Everyone jumped and*
> *came running in time to see Paddle plunge over the edge.*

When we stood at the actual setting, even without seeing anything go over the falls, we internalized a memorable image that perfectly illustrated the inexorable pull of the water to the sea, the central notion of Holling's book.

It was the vintage Maid of the Mists sight-seeing boat ride, though, that put us right in the middle of the book's full-page picture of the falls and another of the little boat turned upside down and shooting across the face of a gigantic wave. The Maid of the Mists boats are good-size vessels, each carrying scores of tourists, but the falls are so colossal (and the thundering so loud at the churning base of the falls, where the boat hovers for ten minutes) that we both felt, from that vantage point, almost as small relative to nature as that carved Indian boy.

The Itinerary

Niagara Falls can, of course, be visited from either the American or the Canadian side. Each side has its kitschy tourist attractions, like wax museums and motels with heart-shape beds, and each side has parklands bordering the falls, although the parklands are more extensive on the Canadian side. (And U.S. travelers should note that there may be more frequent and convenient flights into Toronto than into Buffalo, New York.) Maid of the Mists rides originate on both sides, and it's easy to cross back and forth between Ontario and New York to see specific attractions.

Approaching Niagara Falls from the Canadian side is quite a stirring experience because your sense of their immensity and power increases gradually. At first, you might dismiss this wonder of the world as not such a big deal, but by the end of a string of obligatory sight-seeing stops, you will not remain cynical or unawed. We began by driving along the parklands above the falls and seeing, at the same level as the road we were driving on, the rushing water of the Niagara River flowing downstream toward the chasm. Next, we went to the Table Top lookout and peered over the edge of Horseshoe Falls from the top before taking an elevator down to viewpoints behind the falls.

Finally, we went, as all good tourists do, to ride a Maid of the Mists boat, and I'm here to tell you there's no point in visiting Niagara Falls, with or without kids, if you're not going to ride this boat. It's an elemental thrill. You walk down to the dock, are handed a disposable waterproof poncho, and position yourself along with other camera-toting visitors at the deck railing. The boat motors for five minutes toward Horseshoe Falls, and then, when you're close enough to be gazing up at a mountain of water, it seems to stop. Although it no longer makes headway, the boat continues to push against the current while the falls push back—effectively suspending motion for ten minutes while the crashing waters roar all around you and the constant mist pours down like rain.

Irene and I signed up for a guided day tour (which also included a buffet lunch at a hotel restaurant with spectacular views) that had us on and off a bus between stops that were actually within walking distance of each other. It continued after the boat ride for a drive on the scenic Niagara Parkway along the bluffs of the river below the falls. It was a handy way to see the area, but our woefully (almost comically) unin formed driver-guide didn't add anything to our knowledge of the area. A self-tour by car would be just as easy.

On the American side, Goat Island is a wooded area with paved pathways that allow another view from the top of the falls, with Horseshoe Falls to one side and Bridal Veil Falls to another. It's where you can, in the summer, go down wooden walkways (the Cave of the Winds trip) almost to the base of the falls.

About an hour away on the Canadian side is the quaintly restored nineteenth-century village of Niagara-on-the-Lake. It's full of souvenir shops, ice cream parlors, and bakeries, and has a pretty little beachside park. Irene and I made a point on our visit of walking down to the beach and looking out across Lake Ontario at the distinctive skyline of Toronto, the next stop on Paddle's trip.

JOURNEYS THROUGH TIME AND SPACE

In several books in addition to *Paddle-to-the-Sea*, Holling uses a similar device to help the young reader follow along on a sweeping geographical or historical journey. *Minn of the Mississippi* is about a snapping turtle who swims from the source to the mouth of the Mississippi River; it traces not only the turtle's life cycle, but also the history and changing geography of the river. *Tree in the Trail* and *Seabird* offer journeys through time. The first tells the story of the Santa Fe Trail by describing events in the vicinity of a cottonwood tree that's protected from buffalo by an Indian boy, then, as it grows, sees the passage of, successively, explorers, hunters, trappers, and settlers. *Seabird* ranges through time *and* space, teaching American maritime history by following a carved ivory gull from a whaling ship off Nantucket, to Pacific and Yankee clippers, to steamships in the '20s. ✂ The girl's classic in this genre is *Hitty: Her First Hundred Years*, a Newbery Award-winner by Rachel Field, told by a wooden doll who is carved in a farmhouse in Maine, travels on a whaling ship to India, and, after many adventures, ends up in an antiques store in New York.

Names and Numbers

On the Canadian side:
Niagara Falls Tourism
5515 Stanley St.
Niagara Falls, Ontario,
    Canada
(800) 563-2557
www.discoverniagara.com

On the American side:
Niagara Falls Convention
    and Visitors Bureau
310 4th St.
Niagara Falls, New York
(800) 421-5223
www.nfcvb.com

The Pied Piper of Hamelin (1888)

BY ROBERT BROWNING

Hamelin, Germany

*T*he small German city of Hamelin would be an excellent adventure even without its local legend, but the mysterious tale gives everyone, young and old, a solid way to imagine the European past that's so visible in the ancient buildings and cobblestone streets. Its well-preserved medieval center is only one of the genuinely special aspects of a town that's a good stop on a trip introducing kids to northern Europe. —SLT

This trip is ideal for families with readers between the ages of 7 and 13 and older siblings.

The Poem

The story of the Pied Piper of Hamelin or, in German, *der Rattenfanger von Hameln,* is one of the West's most enduring and tragic mysteries. What happened on June 26, 1284? What became of the 130 children who were enticed away by a piper? Experts today suggest that nothing nefarious occurred, but rather that 130 "children of the town" (as medieval city residents were called then) emigrated as workers to another part of Germany.

But authors—from the Dominican friar Heinrich von

Herford, who wrote in 1450, to the sixteenth-century Aelarius Erich, to the Grimm Brothers, to Robert Browning, whose nineteenth-century poem is the classic account known to English-speakers—have more imagination than experts, and the tale they tell is compelling and unforgettable.

Browning wrote his version for Willy Macready, a young friend who was sick. It's hard to imagine this story cheering anyone up, but its appeal is based on the fact that children encounter many mysteries, including many tragic mysteries, in real life, and legends with some complexity and wonder are the stories that measure up to real life. The tale is a powerful one, probably more disturbing for adults who ponder the unknown fate of the children than for children reading it. In Browning's version, the piper, upon ridding the town of rats and not being paid, leads the children into a cavern in a mountain that closes behind them. The hope is held out that the children survived, because "in Transylvania there's a tribe" whose mothers and fathers had "risen out of some subterraneous prison."

The poem, like many classics, is best read aloud together. Its rhyme scheme is lively, and its use of archaic words is minimal, but clarifying a few points as the plot unfolds makes all the difference in comprehension. It's good to know what a guilder is as the mayor negotiates with the Ratcatcher, for example, and it helps to understand exactly what is in the kegs of salted sprats (herring). A brief explanation of the reason for a walled city (not obvious to today's kids) is helpful, too, but the power play by the town council when they decide *not* to pay the piper will probably be very clear to most kids.

Kids have much to absorb in this tale: the historic reality of rat-infested cities (those are powerful and scary images alone), the morality tale of honoring bargains, the political satire of Browning's description of a mayor "when at noon his paunch grew mutinous—for a plate of turtle, green and glutinous."

And there's the ratcatcher himself, whose famous colorful "quaint attire" was already old-fashioned in the Middle Ages of the tale. He looked to one onlooker, says Browning, as if his "great-grandsire had walked this way from his painted tombstone." There's also the fun of the seldom-mentioned passage about the one rat who survives the plunge into the river Weser and makes it home to rat land, where he tells the tale of the wondrous sound of the pipe whose music sounded like a voice saying, "Munch on, crunch on!"

(In addition to the Browning poem, many fine interpretations/adaptations in English can be found, including a recent version retold and illustrated by Mercer Mayer.)

The Experience

A crowd of German schoolkids laughed and skipped along behind the oddly dressed man playing the clarinet, and although 13-year-old Irene rolled her eyes at the obviousness of it, we followed along, too. Michael Wolper, employed by the Hamelin tourist office to play *der Rattenfanger* (the ratcatcher), embodied the impish spirit of the legendary Pied Piper as he strolled through pedestrianized Old Town in his yellow horned shoes, red and yellow (pied) tunic with long medieval sleeves, and dashing cap with a three-foot-long pheasant feather bobbing in time to his tune. Catching sight of him as they emerged from a shop, a grandmother and child laughed and pointed, and tourists quickly raised their cameras.

At the edge of a large open plaza, the piper hurried off to head the cast of the pageant that is put on by the town on summer Sundays. Scores of families joined the schoolchildren we'd followed and made themselves comfy on benches or simply on the cobblestones as the children of Hamelin, in full-length rat suits, made their entrance.

The pageant isn't professional at all, and that's what makes it charming—children watching children dressed as rats, retelling a legend based on events that took place more than eight hundred years ago. And although there are a few souvenir shops (gummy rats, rat candles), the town is geared as much to local weekenders as to an international jet-setting tourist crowd, and the stores run the gamut of gift, fashion, and sundries outlets. As we watched the performance, adults also admired the plaza's remarkable Weser Renaissance buildings, with their intricately carved polychrome details of fantastic figures. Children simply hung out, enjoying the sunshine and the show.

Afterward, Irene and I joined the entire population of the town for ice cream. Ice cream cafés in Germany are mostly seasonal, run by Italians who arrive in the spring and leave in the fall. On this sunny day, the ice cream cafés were filled to capacity, every outdoor table jammed with customers, and so we stepped into the cool, shady interior of one of the cafés and watched the waitresses run back and forth while the countermen created elaborate sundaes. Glancing at the menu, we saw that food was served there as well, but we passed over the spaghetti and pizza and ordered dishes with *Schokolade* and *Karamel*.

"Look, Mom, he's putting the ice cream through the pasta maker!" Irene said, and we discovered what the "spaghetti" on this menu really was. "Noodles" of vanilla ice cream were topped with strawberry syrup and something that looked like Parmesan but must have been finely ground nuts. As we enjoyed our own cold, creamy treats, we counted a dozen ice-cream spaghettis rushed to waiting kids.

The Itinerary

Hamelin is the family-friendliest town along Germany's much-promoted Fairy Tale Road, so it would be a satisfying stop with kids even without the literary connection. One of the few German cities whose historic buildings survived World War II, Hamelin has a gem of an old town that is noted for the richly decorated facades of its seventeenth- and eighteenth-century half-timbered buildings. On the more practical side, the extensive pedestrian area means parents can let little ones move around without fearing vehicle traffic.

A short train ride from Hanover, Hamelin is a day trip for many international visitors, but we recommend stopping at least overnight. There is a range of hotels and guest houses, including several in the Old Town area, and an array of cafés and restaurants. (We enjoyed the Pancake [*Pfannekuchen*] House, where more than thirty kinds of latkes, crepes, and griddle cakes are offered in a wonderfully rustic, low-ceilinged half-timbered house.)

The modest but fascinating museum shouldn't be missed. Skip the ground-floor exhibits of German folk art and furniture and go instead to the upstairs hall, where a rotating series of shows always offers some slant on the Pied Piper legend. There's a case of Pied Piper books in every language, and we saw a wonderful exhibit explaining what real-life medieval ratcatchers did. We won't soon forget the historically accurate life-size model of a ratcatcher with tame critters on one shoulder and little rat corpses hanging from a pole he carried over the other shoulder.

More than eighty local actors (including dozens of children costumed as rats) perform in the weekly summertime retelling of the Pied Piper. The half-hour play is staged Sundays at noon between mid-May and mid-September on the terrace of the seventeenth-century Hochzeitshaus, which is also the location of daily glockenspiel "performances" of the story (1:05, 3:35, and 5:35 P.M.).

Hourly boat excursions on the Weser River, a glassworks factory with a gallery for watching glass blown freehand, the fountain in Pferdemarkt where kids control the water spouting (a delight on a hot summer afternoon), and perhaps a castle visit—there are ten castles within a ninety-minute drive from Hamelin—round out the activities for families.

Names and Numbers

German National Tourist
  Office
122 E. 42nd St., Chanin Bldg,
  52nd floor
New York City
(212) 661-7200
www.germany-tourism.de

German Rail Pass
(800) 782-2424
www.dertravel.com

Hamelin Tourist Information
  Office
Verkehrsverein Hameln
e.V., Deisterallee 3
Hameln
(49) (05151) 202617;
fax (05151) 202500
www.hameln.de/touristinfo

Pfannekuchen (Pancake)
  House
Hummenstrasse 12
Hameln
(05151) 41378

Mosena Ice Cream Parlor
Osterstrasse 10
Hameln

Ramona Quimby, Age 8 (1981)
& Other Titles

BY BEVERLY CLEARY

Portland, Oregon

A visit to lush, damp Portland will be brightened for any fan of Ramona Quimby and Henry Huggins by a trip to Klickitat Street and nearby Grant Park, home of the Beverly Cleary Sculpture Garden. Portland is also a city full of good libraries, most notably (for our purposes) the Beverly Cleary Children's Library, tucked inside the great Central Library downtown. —CDB

This trip is ideal for families with readers between the ages of 8 and 11.

The Books

In a memoir, Beverly Cleary wrote:

Writing for young readers was my childhood ambition. . . . I had had enough of books about wealthy English children who had nannies and pony carts or books about poor children whose problems were solved by a long-lost rich relative turning up in the last chapter. I wanted to read funny stories about the sort of children I knew, and I decided that someday when I grew up I would write them.

One day she did, in fact, grow up, and in 1949, at the urging of her husband, the former librarian and then stay-at-home mom finally sat down to write. The result was a funny book about a realistic boy named Henry Huggins. That first book, *Henry Huggins,* was published in 1950, launching a career in children's literature that has spanned generations. Children everywhere responded to her honest, amusing stories about real children, and over the last five decades, she has kept the books coming; the latest, *Ramona's World,* was published in 1999.

As she wrote, Cleary gradually developed the characters who lived in Glenwood, the name she gave the neighborhood of her youth. (By then she lived in California, and she's still there.) It started with Henry, the boy who lives on Klickitat Street. His good friend, Beezus Quimby, has a pesky little sister named Ramona; they also live on Klickitat. Sometimes when Mrs. Quimby is working, Ramona and Beezus go home from school with Howie and his little sister, Willa Jean. Henry Huggins eventually gets a dog, Ribsy, who becomes a force to be reckoned with. A few blocks away live the protagonists of other Cleary books, notably Ellen Tebbits and Otis Spofford.

All these kids are regular kids to whom kids today still completely relate. They are not the plucky pioneers enduring unimaginable hardships, the rich children with ponies and nannies, or the impossibly poor children who discover they have a rich grandfather. They are kids who go to their neighborhood school, squabble with siblings, love their parents, annoy their parents, get paper routes, worry when their parents lose their jobs, plan birthday parties, deal with classroom humiliations, cope with lots of rainy days, try to keep a mischievous dog out of trouble (Henry), try to get their father to quit smoking (Ramona and Beezus), and generally go about the business of being kids.

Even now, well into old age, Cleary has a razor-sharp memory for what it feels like to be 9 years old. She knows how to convey the humor in everyday situations, and she allows her characters to be honest—sometimes they're brave and caring, other times they're frightened and deceitful. Which is why, all across America, there are 9-year-olds right this minute who are reading their way through the entire Beverly Cleary library.

The Experience

Erin fell in love with Ramona and Beezus Quimby, Henry Huggins, and Ribsy the dog at age 8½ and she spent the next year reading every book in which they appeared, as well as almost all of Beverly Cleary's other books. No matter that by the time we went to Portland, she was 11 and had since moved on to the Harry Potter books, the Roald Dahl books, and the Anastasia Krupnik books—she was still eager to see the real Klickitat Street.

When we arrived it wasn't raining, but this being Oregon, we knew the situation could change at any moment, and we wanted to enjoy Grant Park without storm gear. So we got settled quickly and hurried over to Northeast Portland. We drove north on 33rd Street past Grant Park, and a few blocks later we found Klickitat Street. The fictional Quimby and Huggins families lived on this street, in the same neighborhood as the real Beverly Cleary (then Beverly Bunn) did in the 1920s and '30s. As we headed east on Klickitat, we passed through a few blocks that Erin deemed far too ritzy for her fictional friends. Then the houses shrank to middle-class proportions, and we passed kids on scooters, kids on trikes, and kids manning a lemonade stand.

"That's it! That's Ramona's house," Erin said with authority.

It was just a basic one-story house, with white siding, a screen door, and a small yard—an ordinary house for an ordinary family whose ordinary lives Cleary made witty and absorbing.

We stopped at a kid-sponsored garage sale a block further up Klickitat, splurged on a fifty-cent gift for the left-at-home little sister, and headed back to Grant Park, which Cleary called Glenwood Park in her books. Near the playground, we spotted a bronze, slightly larger-than-life Henry Huggins off to the right. We'd found it: the Beverly Cleary Sculpture Garden. Erin raced over, climbed on Ribsy, and begged for photo after photo to be taken of her with Ramona and Henry. She hopped from engraved stone to engraved stone. *"Ramona and Her Father*—read that," she said. *"Henry and Beezus*—read that. *Ellen Tebbits*— read that." And on through every Cleary book set in Portland, each one memorialized in a stone square set into the ground.

The sculptures thoroughly explored and fussed over, Erin then moved to the adjacent playground, full of the same joy that Ramona exudes in her bronze incarnation: head back, big smile, hair sticking up. Erin ran, swung, climbed, and slid. Sure enough, it started drizzling, but she kept on swinging. Ramona and Henry, after all, never let a little rain slow them down.

The Itinerary

Portland is a great city for families. It has OMSI, a science museum loved for its planetarium and real submarine. It has the Children's Museum of Portland, newly expanded and moved to the former waterfront OMSI site. It has the great Saturday Market (held on Sundays, too), an extraordinary outdoor craft market with food, music, and entertainers. It has the Oregon Zoo, the annual Rose Festival, the run-through Salmon Street Springs fountains in Tom McCall Waterfront Park, and, not far out of town, the Oregon Caves.

Portland also has an innate bookishness, typically attributed to the city's unusual number of rainy days. That bookishness makes it easy for families to have a literary focus to a Portland stay. And what better focal point than Beverly Cleary's Portland books? After all, given the still-broad appeal of these books (many of which were written in the '50s and '60s), you're likely to have a Cleary fan if you have a child over the age of 8.

The heart of your kid-lit Portland experience will be the visit to Cleary's old neighborhood, especially Klickitat Street and Grant Park. Cleary's family moved to this neighborhood when she was 6 years old, and she lived here until she fled the rain to attend college in California. When she began writing children's books, she set them in her old neighborhood (to which she gave the fictional name Glenwood), and settled both Ramona's and Henry's families on Klickitat. It's just a regular Portland residential street, with tidy houses, pretty gardens, and ordinary people. Grant Park, a verdant 20-acre spread next to Grant High School (which Cleary attended), has all the worthy city-park amenities: baseball fields, basketball and tennis courts, open lawns, trees, and a playground. It also has the Beverly Cleary Sculpture Garden, featuring slightly-larger-than-life bronze statues of Ramona, Henry, and Ribsy, created by artist Lee Hunt. Engraved stones set in the ground commemorate every Cleary book set in Portland, and in the summer, from time to time, water shoots out of the ground, turning the sculpture garden into a fountain.

Another Lee Hunt work, a bust of Ramona, is on display in the children's room at the Gresham Regional Library, about 10 miles north of Grant Park, but it's not particularly worth a special trip out of town. Instead, to continue your bookish tour of Portland, head downtown to the Beverly Cleary Children's Library, which is tucked inside the grand old Central Library. It doesn't have Ramona art, but it does have a handsome wall sculpture of Alice in Wonderland and a cool, hands-on Tree of Knowledge sculpture engraved with all sorts of children's-book references. It's a wonderful place to hang out on a rainy Portland afternoon. Later, if the skies are dry, you can head down to the banks of the Willamette River to Waterfront Park, a beautiful twenty-two-block-long urban park, and look for the Children's Story Garden, where stories, riddles, and pictures are carved into granite tiles, which are set into a maze format that's fun to navigate. (Hint: It's at the north end of the park.)

When souvenir time comes (as it always does with kids), there's only one place to go: Powell's, the world's largest bookstore. An incredible number of inexpensive used books are filed right alongside the new, so with luck you can round out your Beverly Cleary library and still have money left for a grown-up book or two, along with treats for everyone in the coffeehouse. It's a vast and awe-inspiring place in which you can wander for hours, or days—or, as many native Portlanders know, for years and years.

Names and Numbers

Grant Park
N.E. 33rd Ave. & U. S.
    Grant Pl.
Portland
(503) 823-PLAY
www.multnomah.lib.or.us/
    lib/kids/cleary.html
    (sculpture garden details)

Beverly Cleary Children's
    Library
Multnomah County Central
    Library
801 S.W. 10th Ave.
Portland
(503) 988-5123
www.multnomah.lib.or.us/
    lib/kids

Tom McCall Waterfront Park
Front St. from Clay St. to
  N.W. Glisan St.
Portland
(503) 823-PLAY

Powell's City of Books
1005 W. Burnside
Portland
(503) 228-0540
www.powells.com
*Also check out
www.beverlycleary.com, the
official Beverly Cleary Web
site, which includes an
interactive map of Cleary's
neighborhood.*

Song of the Swallows (1948)

BY LEO POLITI

San Juan Capistrano, California

*F*ounded in 1776, Mission San Juan Capistrano is one of the loveliest in the chain of California missions—and it's also one of the best suited for children, thanks in part to Leo Politi's storybook. Often called the "Jewel of the Missions," San Juan Capistrano has been internationally famous since the 1930s for the annual return of migrating swallows. The historic, friendly little mission town is an ideal stop for many traveling families: Orange County's southern beaches are just a few minutes to the south, and Disney's parks are about thirty minutes to the north.   —CDB

This trip is ideal for families with readers between the ages of 6 and 10, and older siblings will appreciate the mission.

The Book

Although he was born to an Italian immigrant family, Leo Politi focused several of his children's books on California's Latino culture. As a young artist, he set up his easel on L.A.'s Olvera Street, where he felt most at home. Sadly, many of Politi's books are now out of print—but the one that remains popular is one of his best. *Song of the Swallows* won the Caldecott Medal in 1950, for Politi's gentle, joyous illustrations of the mission's gardens, the swallows, the church bells, and the young boy, Juan, who loves the gardens, the bell ringer, and the swallows.

The tale is a simple one. Juan passes by the mission as he goes to and from school every day. During his frequent visits he becomes friends with Julian, the gardener and bell ringer. Julian teaches him about the mission and its history, and together they marvel at the swallows flying in and out of their mud houses in the mission's tile-covered eaves. (Julian tells Juan that the swallows spend the winter on a magical island in the Pacific, though we now know that they actually go to a town in Argentina.) Juan cares for a lost baby swallow and considers the birds to be his dear friends. When they leave in the fall, he is very sad, until he turns this sadness around by doing something to welcome the swallows back in the spring: He plants a garden in the front of his house, in hopes that his flowers and pool of water will attract them.

Come spring, Juan joins the local schoolchildren in the annual March 19 fiesta of the swallows. Hour after hour, the swallows don't come, and by late afternoon many children give up waiting, but Juan remains faithful. Sure enough, the birds come, and he gets to ring the mission bells with Julian. To add to his great joy, when he gets home he discovers that a pair of swallows have nested near his garden. Life is sweet for this little boy.

Good to read aloud to very young children, or for second- and third-graders to read on their own, the book gives just enough history to hold kids' interest, along with an introduction to some basic Spanish words and a feeling for life in old

California. Time spent with this book before a mission visit will add much to the experience.

The Experience

"You mean we have to go to *church?*" said Erin. "On a *Saturday?*" Our outing to Mission San Juan Capistrano was not getting off to a promising start. But once she realized that she could wear play clothes instead of church clothes, and there just might be animals involved, she stopped complaining. (Her younger sister, Emily, had no such complaints, being the sort of child who finds both dressing up and going to church to be fun.)

Because we're a southern California family, the San Juan mission is in our own backyard. In fact, because I spent many childhood weekends at our Capistrano Beach house, and many a childhood Sunday at the Spanish-language Mass at the mission, I'm sentimental about the place. Yet I'd never quite managed to take the kids there, anticipating the exact reaction I got from Erin when I announced our outing. (A mission visit falls under the good-for-you department for most kids.) But at 10, she had reached the age when every California schoolchild learns about Father Junipero Serra and his string of Catholic missionary church-villages. So like it or not, it was time to take the girls inside the place they'd driven past so many times.

Fortunately, once we read *Song of the Swallows*, they were primed for the experience, and it was more fun for all of us than we expected. True, they wouldn't rank it up there with Knott's Berry Farm, but they had a perfectly lovely time sticking their hands in the fountains, looking down the old well, exploring the ancient church cemetery, asking questions of the costumed docents, going into the former soldiers' barracks, buying friendship bracelets from a docent working a spinning wheel, and looking for swallows' nests. They only found three, but that seemed to be plenty.

After a lunch break, we moseyed on down to the other side of the tracks (literally) for a visit to the Jones Family Mini Farm, where we'd been many times before, to feed the rabbits and goats and have a pony ride. We were pleased to discover a new attraction: a ride on a covered hay wagon, pulled by a tractor, through the surrounding historic neighborhood. It was hokey, yes, but the kids are still young enough to love hokey, and the driver's narrative of San Juan's early rancho and mission days enriched the ride.

The Itinerary

Swallows week is the time to visit San Juan if you want to join in the annual celebration of the returning swallows. The festivities bracket St. Joseph's Day, March 19, the day the birds have traditionally returned from their winter home in Argentina— although they might start showing up on the 15th or the 25th, and some years only a few show up at all.

Back in Juan's day (the book doesn't give a time period, but it looks like the early part of the twentieth century), the mission and the then-tiny town of San Juan were surrounded by rich valley farmland. Rich farmland meant lots of bugs, so word got out in the swallow world that the eating was good— not to mention that the eaves of the adobe mission buildings made perfect nesting spots. Today, the farmland has largely been replaced by housing tracts, so the bugs, and therefore the swallows, are far fewer. And because there are more houses, there are more eaves for nest building, so the ones that do come are more dispersed. The mission is doing its part to lure the birds home, via a huge release of ladybugs in mid-March and the construction of faux ceramic nests to make the swallows think that lots of other swallows have already made camp. The weekend before St. Joseph's Day is dubbed Swallows Weekend, and it's always filled with family-oriented amusements: Native American dancers, mariachis, *ballet folklorico*, living-history actors, traditional craft workers (spinners, blacksmiths, etc.), Aztec-style face painting, and good Mexican and American food. One lucky kid wins a raffle drawing that lets him or her ring the mission bells that welcome the swallows.

The Saturday after the 19th of March is devoted to the Los Golondrinas (*golondrinas* is Spanish for "swallows") parade, billed as the largest nonmotorized parade in the West. It's tremendously popular with locals, given that it showcases things like Brownie troops, junior-high marching bands, schoolkids dressed like birds and Spanish padres, and hairiest-man contests. It has a small-town wackiness that's a lot of fun for kids.

If you visit anytime after the annual shindig, you'll find the town quieter and the parking easier. (The swallows stick around until October, when they head back to Argentina.) And if you're coming from Los Angeles, San Diego, or many points in between, consider visiting San Juan by train—the town's sights are clustered right around the Amtrak depot, making this a rare California day trip that doesn't require a car. (Besides, kids love train rides.) A San Juan outing makes a fine detour from a family Disney trip, because the Anaheim train station is just a couple of stops north.

You can spend a wonderful day in San Juan following in young Juan's footsteps. The walled gardens of the mission look much like Politi's 1948 illustrations, thanks to a major landscaping renovation; kids won't care about the genus of each carefully labeled plant, but they'll enjoy running along the garden paths. Walk around the grounds and keep your eyes upward, looking for the mud houses the swallows build in the eaves. Watch for the other birds Juan loved: pigeons, hummingbirds, and sparrows. Inspect the huge old millstone that Juan sees. Check out the soldiers' barracks he liked to look at. (Have your kids notice how small the cots seem.) And if you're planning to come on a Saturday, call ahead to reserve one of the hands-on workshops for kids, where they can do things like make adobe bricks or weave baskets—they're held every other Saturday, alternating with living-history programs.

When you've had enough of the mission, walk across the street and down Verdugo Street to the old train station. If you didn't arrive via Amtrak, consider hanging around for a spell to watch a train roar into the station, always a thrilling experience for children. Just across the tracks is the Los Rios District, which calls itself the oldest neighborhood in California (ignoring the fact that Indians had neighborhoods, too). It's a short, pleasant walk along shady Los Rios Street, which is lined with two-hundred-year-old houses, some of which look like Juan's little adobe house. If the kids seem interested, you can stop in the O'Neill Museum, a circa-1800 house full of period furnishings and photos and memorabilia from old San Juan.

To end on a child-pleasing high note, stop (as we did) at the Jones Family Mini Farm. It's a sweet little petting farm with pony rides, gentle animals to feed, a choo-choo train ride, and a twenty-minute, $2 hay wagon ride through Los Rios. The farm conveys a hint of the days when this modern suburb was a small agricultural settlement dominated by the old mission.

Names and Numbers

Mission San Juan Capistrano
Camino Capistrano and
   Ortega Hwy.
San Juan Capistrano
(949) 234-1300
Open daily 8:30 A.M.–5 P.M.
www.missionsjc.com

Los Rios District/O'Neill
   Historic Museum
31831 Los Rios St.
San Juan Capistrano
(949) 493-8444
Museum open Tues.–Fri.
9 A.M.–4 P.M. (closed for
lunch).

Jones Family Mini Farm
31791 Los Rios St.
San Juan Capistrano
(949) 831-6550
Open Wed.–Sun. 11 A.M.–
4 P.M. (closed when it rains).

The Tale of Peter Rabbit (1902)
& Other Titles

BY BEATRIX POTTER

The Lake District, England

P oets and painters have long revered this part of the English countryside, and families who spend time in the miniature world of Beatrix Potter will be enchanted by the small-scale beauties of this bucolic land-scape. Leave the high-tech world behind and expect to slow way down to enjoy such sights as bunnies disappearing under hedges, baby lambs frolicking in green meadows, and tiny flowers tucked into the roots of moss-covered tree trunks. —SLT

This trip is ideal for families with readers between the ages of 10 and 13 and their younger siblings.

The Books

Sometimes it seems as if we have children for our own amusement—not just because our children amuse us, but because we, as parents, can then enjoy those delightful entertainments purportedly devised for children. We soon learn that the best children's books, songs, plays, and pictures speak to adults as well, and though we may be interlopers in some ways, we are a necessary part of the experience—our child's guides through magic lands.

So it is with Beatrix Potter stories. We read these to our youngest children, and then the books stay on the shelves within reach for years after regular out-loud story hours are over. But when someone's sick in bed and dipping into old favorites, or when an older child looks about for something to read to a visiting cousin, then Squirrel Nutkin and Benjamin Bunny and, of course, Peter Rabbit make their appearance. For every age reader, Potter's nuances and subtleties of text and drawing, as well as her frankly humorous point of view, make these animal stories a memorable chapter of English literature.

"Oh, yes, if you please'm," says Miss Tiggy Winkle in a phrase that echoes often in my mind, while friends can recite much of *The Tale of Peter Rabbit* ("Flopsy, Mopsy, and Cottontail, who were good little bunnies, went down the lane to gather blackberries . . .") by heart. The picture of Hunca Munca the mouse sitting next to a stolen doll cradle with her baby in her lap is an image that will never leave me, and my daughter still lingers long over the picture of Lucie looking up as she climbs a stile at a hill that disappears in the clouds.

When her first book was published, Beatrix Potter was 35, the dutiful but determined daughter of wealthy but austere parents. The runaway success of *The Tale of Peter Rabbit,* which sold fifty thousand copies in two years, and the steady sales of her subsequent books, including *The Tale of Squirrel Nutkin* (1903) and *The Tailor of Gloucester* (1903), allowed her to purchase large tracts of land in the Lake District, Cumbria, where her family had often vacationed. There, at Hill Top Farm and other properties, she went into business as a farmer, raising sheep and other animals with the help of a supervisor, and splitting her time between Cumbria and London. After her marriage to a local barrister, she lived full time in the Lake District, and the books after 1906 are often clearly set in the area. *The Tale of Mr. Jeremy Fisher* (1906) takes place on a lake near her farm. *Jemima Puddle Duck* was based on a restless waterfowl of Ms. Potter's acquaintance, and other books, including *The Tale of Tom Kitten, The Tale of Samuel Whiskers,* and *The Tale of Ginger and Pickles,* depict the animals, landmarks, and people of the village of Near Sawrey and vicinity.

The Experience

The scene in the Lake District seemed to bring out the artist in each of us. It was Easter morning. Irene and I sat in rustic twig chairs on the misty banks of Coniston Water. The lake was undisturbed by ripples or waves, and the mist rising from its glassy surface softened the outlines of sailboats and trees. To Irene's right, twin lambs stuck inquisitive faces over a low fence rail, then turned at the sound of their mother's bleat and trotted to her side.

Irene, whose right leg was encased in a "moonboot" to sta-bilize a slight ankle fracture, sat contentedly for more than an hour, sketching with the colored pencils she'd bought the day before at the Armitt Museum in Ambleside. We had stopped in to see the Beatrix Potter exhibit, which turned out to be a quiet revelation for my middle-schooler. After seeing a display of Potter's colorful, meticulous paintings of fungi of the region (like chanterelle mushrooms and hairy bracket fungus), and another exhibit showing an arrangement of art supplies and sketches on a desk that had belonged to Potter, Irene started thinking not only about Peter Rabbit and Miss Tiggy Winkle, but also about the scientist (for Potter was a committed natu-ralist) and artist who created them.

That Easter morning, as Irene sketched, I reacquainted myself with the self-timer on the camera and took a picture of us. Then I took another picture of the lake and the mysterious play of reflection and fog and light. Then I took pictures of flowers and sheep.

It's easy to wander around besotted in the Lake District. If I'd had a tape recorder with me, I would have taped the steady sound of the countryside that rose around us that morning. It was as if some overwrought sound-effects engineer had stuffed a soundtrack full of bird twitters, water tumbling in a stream, and sheep baaing—followed by a woodpecker and, in too-close-to-be-real succession, a lamb's bleat, a dove's coo, and an insect's whirring wings.

But foremost in my mind that morning was the thought that Beatrix Potter had not only treasured and been inspired by scenes like the ones my daughter and I were enjoying, but actually preserved them for our pleasure and inspiration—in reality as well as in her books. The Lake District exists largely because of Potter's farsighted efforts as one of the earliest major land donors to the National Trust. She not only gave land but also managed enormous sheep farms to preserve local breeds until the Trust could administer those efforts. The unique part-wild, part-domestic landscape, with its pastures, stone fences, narrow roads, and spectacular hills, owes much to her efforts.

Going to Hill Top, the farm Potter bought with proceeds from *The Tale of Peter Rabbit,* Irene and I felt as if we'd entered an incredible shrinking machine. From the small-scale charm (with plenty of holiday hustle and bustle) of the area's larger villages, we drove to an even smaller hamlet called Near Sawrey, a curve in the road with a few whitewashed buildings and a crossroads that still looks exactly as it did when it figured in the background of a picture of two well-dressed pigs in *The*

Tale of Pigling Blandings. Then we walked down the road to an even smaller setting, the entrance to the farm.

Only a handful of people are allowed into the cottage at a time, to prevent overcrowding, so we arrived before opening and were among the first visitors of the day. You park in a tiny lot, then walk to the farm's entrance, where a gatehouse combines the functions of ticket booth and shop. You pass through the gatehouse and then walk down a garden path to the small farmhouse with its half dozen or so rooms.

With an inexpensive but very helpful illustrated souvenir booklet in hand, we strolled through the garden and cottage, noting that the rhubarb patch found its way into *Jemima Puddle Duck,* the Hill Top porch is depicted in *The Tale of Tom Kitten,* and the kitchen is seen in *The Tale of Samuel Whiskers.* Docents posted in the cottage showed us how the parlor is sketched into *The Tale of the Pie and the Patty-Pan,* and most memorably, they showed us Potter's nineteenth-century dollhouse and accessories (including plaster food) that were so faithfully rendered in *The Tale of Two Bad Mice.*

It was an illuminating walk through a very small, personal literary landmark, and it could be a child's first lesson in how an artist makes the everyday immortal.

The Itinerary

The drive into the Lake District can be daunting—off the highways and onto country roads that wind up and down the mountains. For Americans, steering to the left while avoiding the stone walls that border many roads is a challenge that can fray tempers after two hours or so. So even if you plan a brief visit, allow one or two overnights in the district, and know that sometimes you'll be driving for hours behind pokey sightseers or farm vehicles. And, more enjoyably, allow time to take a country walk between one village and another (a path that begins at Hill Top Farm meanders over stiles and through pastures, for example).

A visit to Beatrix Potter's farm is really best as part of a longer holiday in the Lake District, a region that offers plenty of English country fun for families. If you're visiting during a quieter time (spring, fall, midweek), Hawkshead (and an adjacent green-meadow campground) can be a pleasant base. Of course, there are B&Bs and country hotels scattered throughout the Lake District. A room in Coniston, Windermere, or Ambleside puts you within easy reach (a fifteen-minute drive) of Hill Top.

Other area attractions run the gamut from literary landmarks to pottery workshops, historic houses to hiking trails, waterfalls to working farms. Among the family amusements are a cruise on Coniston Water in an 1859 steam yacht, a railway ride through the forest, and a wildlife center. It's really a full-service holiday area, with beaches and sailing and every kind of shop and café scattered among the dozen main villages and the eighteen smaller hamlets.

For the youngest children, just hanging out at the bed-and-breakfast will probably bring home the Beatrix Potter experience. Everywhere you look there are tabby cats sitting on quaint garden walls, Jemima Puddle Ducks waddling toward a pond's edge, Jeremy Frogs croaking in the reeds, and for the lucky, even the occasional Peter Rabbit peering from a hollow tree. The view from any picnic table is likely to be of storybook perfection: green pastures dotted with tiny white daisies, stone fences stretching up hillsides, trees—some majestic, some dear—and, everywhere in the spring, gamboling lambs. Birdsongs are so varied and incredible that my daughter and I began to understand why the Brits go on about this sort of thing in poetry.

A stop at the Beatrix Potter Gallery in Hawkshead can be rewarding, because the changing exhibits of her original drawings and paintings offer both familiar favorites and surprises. Hawkshead, a village of considerable charm, is strained to the bursting point during the busiest times of the year. The parking lot seems to hold more cars than the village holds people, and during peak times all the commercial activity—shops stuffed chockablock with Potter-themed china, pillows, books, and every imaginable what-have-you—completely overwhelms Potter's delicate artistic legacy.

But Irene and I simply walked up the cobblestone street to the Hawkshead country churchyard, where, on a bench amid eighteenth-century tombstones interspersed with daffodils, we sat quietly and looked out over the village, farms, and mountains beyond. The spirit of Beatrix Potter was immediately on the rise again, striding off in long skirts and sturdy shoes along the muddy path below us.

Names and Numbers

British Tourist Authority
551 5th Ave., 7th floor
New York City
(877) 899-8391
(800) 462-2748
www.visitbritain.com
www.travelbritain.org

The National Trust
North West Regional Office
The Hollens, Grasmere
Ambleside, Cumbria
(44) (15394) 35599
www.nationaltrust.org.uk

Beatrix Potter Gallery
Main St., Hawkshead
Ambleside, Cumbria
(44) (15394) 36355

Hill Top
2 miles south of Hawkshead
    in Near Sawrey
Ambleside, Cumbria
(44) (15394) 36269

The Armitt Library and
    Museum
Rydal Rd.
Ambleside, Cumbria
(44) (15394) 31212
www.armitt.com

The Watsons Go to Birmingham—1963 (1995)

BY CHRISTOPHER PAUL CURTIS

Birmingham, Alabama

By creating the Civil Rights District around the 16th Street Baptist Church, where four young girls were killed by a segregationist's bomb in 1963, the city of Birmingham honors the brave individuals who struggled against racism in that era. The district encompasses the same neighborhood visited by Kenneth Watson, the 10-year-old protagonist of this much-honored novel. Kenneth is such a vivid, funny, and memorable character that he seems destined to take his place beside Tom, Huck, Anne, Eloise, and others in the pantheon of classic literary kids. —SLT

This trip is ideal for families with readers between the ages of 10 and 13 and their older siblings.

The Book

Kenneth Watson's coming of age is somberly defined by the moment he steps into the 16th Street Baptist Church, shortly after a bomb has exploded, and sees—with his child's unblinking yet uncomprehending eye—the evidence of evil.

But Kenneth makes his way toward and beyond this tragic crossroads in the same way his family makes its journey from

Flint, Michigan, to Birmingham, Alabama, in their 1948 Plymouth—with imagination and humor, and through a childhood that's rich with affection and singularity.

Kenneth is the bright child in his family, a reader so gifted his teacher has him turn the book upside down to slow him down when he reads aloud. His Birmingham-born mother, Wilona, talks "southern-style" when she gets angry, and bundles up her kids so much in the winter that Kenneth has to help his little sister Joetta get unwrapped when they get to school. Wilona complains about "living in an icebox" to her charismatic workingman husband, Daniel, who in turn teases her about the life she might have led down in the segregated South if she'd married Hambone Henderson instead of him.

Kenneth's brother, Byron, is 13 and therefore "officially a teenage juvenile delinquent." Byron has flunked one grade, and he gets in trouble with his mother for lighting matches while he plays war games in the bathroom. When Byron conks his hair, his wise, worried parents realize that the teen is struggling with racial identity issues, but they don't budge in their determination to guide him as they see fit. Dad not only shaves Byron's head (definitely not a hip style in those days), but the Watson parents also make plans to take the family down to Birmingham for a vacation. Only Byron won't come back—he'll spend the summer away from urban temptations in the care of Grandma Sands. The kids, according to Kenneth, "had heard so many horrible stories about how strict Grandma Sands was . . . the thought of living with her was so terrible that your brain would throw it out as soon as it came in."

In Birmingham, the family is welcomed into the loving arms of Grandma Sands, "a teeny-weeny, old, old, old woman that looked just like Momma would if someone shrank her down about five sizes and sucked all the juice out of her!"

They meet Grandma's friend, Mr. Roberts, and his ancient coon dog, they try to get used to the southern style of talking, and they go swimming at a lake. Kenneth ignores all warnings and swims in an area known for whirlpools. He's sucked under, and as he struggles frantically to get to shore, he realizes with horror that he's being pulled under by an evil gray monster, the Wool Pooh, a character his brother has invented. Then, just as it seems he will drown, he has a vision of Byron leaping into the water with him and fighting off the terrible Wool Pooh. Kenneth has, in fact, been saved by his brother.

The boys don't tell the adults about Kenneth's near-death experience, and so it's thought that his weakness and lassitude for the next few days are because of the heat. And when, on a Sunday morning, the shocking sound of an explosion is heard and "a river of scared brown bodies" starts running from his grandmother's street toward the church, Kenneth is still in a sort of half-conscious state. As people shout and scream and point and yell, he walks in a daze down the street, to the church, and into the Sunday-school area to look for his little sister. Through the smoke and dust he sees signs of carnage that he can't bring himself to understand, and then, looming through the chaos, he sees the big, square shoulders and faceless hulk of the Wool Pooh monster.

The Experience

From my secret hiding place in the living room I could listen to Momma and Dad and it seemed like they spent most of the time trying to figure out how they could explain to us what happened. Some of the time they were mad, some of the time they were calm, and some of the time they just sat on the couch and cried.

Children are often a part of, and witness to, the most dramatic and traumatic moments of history. There's never an "Adults Only" label on times of violent conflict, natural disaster, and other upheaval. That's how it was with the civil rights movement and the hurricane of events that took place in Birmingham, Alabama, in the late 1950s and early '60s. From the teenage Freedom Riders, whose Greyhound bus was firebombed when it pulled into the city, to the eight hundred juveniles, many quite young, arrested during a peaceful demonstration, to the four girls killed and two blinded in the church bombing, children were involved in the struggle at every stage. Many of the battles, of course, were about children. Where and with whom children would go to school was the fundamental political question of the day.

On the sunny spring morning when we visited the Civil Rights District, the teens and preteens in our little group were respectful but not expectant as we walked around Kelly Ingram Park and visited the sanctuary and "memorial nook" of the 16th Street Baptist Church. Along with a busload of teens on a school field trip, they listened politely as older adults spoke of Martin Luther King Jr. and Robert Kennedy and George Wallace. Somewhat dutifully, we trooped into the Civil Rights Institute and watched the film that begins the tour of this interactive, multimedia museum. The film offered an overview of Birmingham history and described how discriminatory laws were gradually introduced and enforced, and how the early civil rights movement was connected to the area's integrated labor unions.

While the school group moved forward through the museum, several of us headed for the rest rooms—where, suddenly, the incredibly personal experience of institutional racism struck home with the kids. Conscious of the adults around them, they whispered among themselves the shocking realization that under segregation they wouldn't have been allowed this simple everyday activity of going to the bathroom together. The act of standing together at the sink and looking into the mirror was now charged with significance.

Kids are mostly quiet as they move through the exhibits at the Civil Rights Institute. In exhibits of advertising images of the '20s and '30s they carefully study racial stereotypes they may have never before seen. They stand in their Nike sportswear intently reading about "the color line in the field" and looking at a photo of 16-year-old Willie Mays with the Birmingham Black Barons. They sign the guest register with great seriousness.

While we were there, none of the kids in the galleries rushed through the exhibits, but instead moved slowly from a picture of Klan children in robes posed under a burning cross, to a video of a demonstration that had taken place on the street corner right outside the museum, to a room where the massive, burned-out front of a Greyhound bus seemed to have just crashed through the wall. From time to time we'd see a young person shake his or her head or point out something to a companion. But there was a lot to take in, including pictures of early '60s college students (neat and pressed in their ties and jackets, skirts and blouses) in workshops preparing for peaceful civil disobedience, an exhibit in which high-pressure fire hoses are turned toward visitors, and a "confrontation gallery" of voices. These last included a child's voice saying, "Negro children should not be allowed to attend white schools," and another wondering, "Am I afraid of the Ku Klux Klan?"

The Itinerary

The Watson family experiences not only a moment in history in Birmingham, but also the contrast between urban and rural life and between northern and southern regional cultures.

Therefore, a visit to Birmingham in the footsteps of Kenneth and his family should include not only the educational and moving experiences of African American historic sites, but also experiences like Kenneth's that are particular to this part of the South.

Birmingham is a vibrant contemporary city, so you're not likely to find, as Kenneth did, slow-moving elders with their ancient coon dogs within the city limits, but you will find sweet tea, "southern-style" talk, hot summer days, and the smell of honeysuckle in the air—and you can take your kids swimming in a lake. Oak Mountain State Park offers a wonderful, close-by experience of the region's natural environment. Just 15 miles south of the city center, it's the state's largest park (10,000 acres) and it preserves a portion of the southernmost part of the Appalachian Mountains. There are campgrounds, picnic areas, hiking, and the fascinating Alabama Wildlife Rehabilitation Center. We recommend a day's visit to swim and picnic at Double Oak Lake and see the injured and orphaned animals recuperating at the wildlife center. One area of the lakefront has a sandy beach, rest rooms, pavilions, and barbecues. You can fish there, too. (But away from the designated swimming area, there are branches poking up from the water and warning signs that you might point out to your kids. Ignoring such a sign was Kenneth's downfall.)

The Civil Rights District includes Kelley Ingram Park, the Birmingham Civil Rights Institute, the 16th Street Baptist Church, the Alabama Jazz Hall of Fame, and the Fourth Avenue Business District, the African American commercial center under segregation. Other notable family attractions in the city include the Alabama Sports Hall of Fame, the Birmingham Zoo, the McWane Center, an interactive science center, and the Sloss Furnaces National Historic Landmark, an unusual museum preserving an enormous pig-iron factory.

Names and Numbers

Birmingham Convention and
  Visitors Bureau
2200 Ninth Ave. North
Birmingham
(800) 458-8085
(205) 458-8000
fax (205) 458-8086
www.birminghamal.org

Birmingham Civil Rights
  Institute
520 16th St. North
Birmingham
(866) 328-9696
(205) 328-9696
fax (205) 323-5219
http://bcri.bham.al.us
Open Tues.–Sat. 10 A.M.–
5 P.M., Sun. 1 P.M.–5 P.M.

Oak Mountain State Park
Accessible from Interstate
  65 at exit 246
(205) 620-2520 or 620-2524
  (park information,
  reservations for picnic
  pavilions or lakeside
  cabins, and fishing
  licenses)
(205) 620-2527 (camping
  reservations)

Alabama Wildlife
  Rehabilitation Center
  and Treetop Nature Trail
(205) 663-7930
www.alawildliferehab.org

Yolonda's Genius (1995)

BY CAROL FENNER

Chicago, Illinois

When the snow melts and the icy winds subside, all of Chicago seems to get outside and celebrate. Perhaps the most joyous celebration of the summer is the Chicago Blues Festival, a four-day party held in downtown's Grant Park. You and your kids can revel in a scene amazingly similar to the one at the climax of *Yolonda's Genius*, when 12-year-old Yolonda maneuvers the crowds, soaks in the music, and finds a way to get her shy little brother up onstage to blow his harmonica with the blues stars. —CDB

This trip is ideal for families with readers between the ages of 10 and 13.

The Book

Not only is Yolonda Blue really smart, but she's also unusually tall and stocky for a 12-year-old—she gets good grades *and* nobody messes with her. She lives in a tough Chicago neighborhood, but she's a tough kid, so it suits her just fine. When her mother announces that they're moving to Grand River, Michigan, Yolonda is miserable. Just because a boy got shot at school, and just because her 6-year-old brother, Andrew, unwittingly accepted a little packet of crack from a junior-high drug dealer, doesn't mean that her mom has to panic and take them out of Chicago!

For Mrs. Blue, a widow and working mom, Grand River is a dream. Here, her paralegal's salary means that instead of a small urban apartment, she can afford a big, pretty house with a garden and a barbecue. The school is safe and good. Yolonda appreciates these things, and even admits that her allowance goes further. But she is miserable nonetheless. For as Fenner writes, "There was no trouble in the air in Grand River—at least no trouble that threatened her life or her lunch money. There was no trouble. There was no nuthin'."

But after a while (and unbeknownst to Mrs. Blue), the kids discover that Grand River has its demons, too. There are still tough kids, and there are still drug dealers. Only here, the kids don't know not to mess with Yolonda or her little brother. Some kids call her "Whale," and no one knows what to make of Andrew, a quiet boy who communicates primarily by playing his harmonica and who is put in a remedial class because he shows no hope of learning to read.

As the story unfolds in this captivating chapter book (good for 10- to 13-year-olds), we follow this African American family through various ups and downs. Yolonda and Andrew each make a friend, they each find a special teacher, and things start to look up. Yolonda knows she's smart, but when someone calls her a "genius," she doesn't know the word. When she looks it up in the dictionary, she realizes that she's just plain smart—it's Andrew, who can't read and who barely talks, who's the genius. She'd always taken it for granted before, but now she sees that his harmonica playing is extraordinary, even magical. This realization makes her more fiercely protective of him than ever.

But then something terrible happens, and Andrew stops playing. As Yolonda tries to figure out how to get him to play again and restore his genius—while also figuring out how to be a friend—the chain of events leads the family back to Chicago to attend the great Blues Festival. They're all overjoyed to visit their former home, to see the Art Institute, the Water Tower, Soldier's Field, Shedd Aquarium, and Lake Michigan again, and to hang out for hours with the crowds in Grant Park, listening to the music that defines their city. It is here, at last, that Yolonda finds a way to make her mother—and all of Chicago—understand her little brother's genius. With Andrew in tow, she cons their way backstage and gets him on the stage, to blow his harmonica with the blues greats. And blow he does.

There are a lot of things to like about this book. Yolonda is a terrific character, and it's a pleasure to watch her learn how to cope with her boundless appetite, her daunting body size, her intelligence, her tough-girl veneer, her desire to both be a rebel loner yet fit in with the cool double-dutch jump rope girls, and her deep love for her sensitive little brother. Her wealthy, vivacious, 300-pound Aunt Tiny is another terrific character. Fenner tells it like it is about drugs, bullies, and school life without getting preachy, and she skillfully conveys both the problems and the glories of Chicago. This complex city provides the perfect backdrop for a book about the complexity of life for a girl on the verge of adolescence, and about the gifted little boy she loves and protects.

The Experience

Because Erin's friend, Garret, 12, was learning to play the bass—in fact, he'd already become a pretty solid bassist—he was champing at the bit to get to the Blues Festival. And because he played an instrument and loved music, he was willing to read a book he'd normally avoid, because it seemed like a girl book. But he was intrigued by the harmonica-playing little brother and ended up quite enjoying the story, especially Andrew's part in it. "Man, that would be so cool to get to meet B. B. King," said Garret. "And to play in front of all those people! I'd probably freak out. But it would be cool."

After Garret's family and mine did the obligatory (and most enjoyable) Lake Michigan boat tour, we trundled over to Grant Park. It was well into the afternoon, and the park was already swarming with people—it wasn't easy for our group of eight to stay together. Our goal was to see Koko Taylor, the queen of Chicago blues, who was that night's headliner, as she was the night Andrew Blue got on stage. (In fact, she's often a headliner, year in and year out.)

Because our group had a couple of little sisters who couldn't handle more than an hour of sitting still at a stretch, we decided to move around as much as possible. First stop was the Juke Joint Stage—we were intrigued by the program notes on its next performer, Johnnie May Dunson Smith, a wheelchair-bound, old-time blues singer and former drummer who'd been evicted from her Chicago home a couple of years earlier. It wasn't too hard to find a spot near the stage, and everyone loved her stage presence, her band, and her powerful voice. The little sisters danced, Garret watched the bass player, and everyone loved her finale, "Big Boss Lady."

Next, we negotiated the lines at a couple of food booths and found a spot to enjoy a feast of smoky ribs and corn roasted in the husk; Garret pointed out that Yolonda ate the same kind of corn. (She eats a lot of different foods in the book, being a girl of very large appetite.) One of the dads took his supper to go and scurried off to try to score seats at the Petrillo Music Shell, while the rest of us took our time and let the kids fool around.

Finally we braved the crowd, waited in the same long

hand-stamp line that slowed down the Blue family, and entered the main concert area. We headed for the eleventh row center, where Yolonda had saved seats, but not surprisingly, there was no sign of *our* seat saver. The place was jammed. And loud: A powerhouse band was putting on a tribute to Howlin' Wolf. We walked back, back, back, until we found our seats. Okay, we wouldn't have Yolonda's view. But the evening was warm, the music was electrifying, and we were going to see Koko Taylor.

She took the stage as darkness began to dominate. The little sisters screamed; Garret and Erin, the big kids, acted cool but wiggled with excitement. Taylor growled and wailed, the crowd cheered, and we felt a part of something bigger than ourselves. Erin was a little disappointed that no lost children appeared on stage that night, but only a little.

"I see why Yolonda didn't want to leave Chicago," said Garret. "This place *jams.*"

The Itinerary

For a *Yolonda's Genius* experience, visit Chicago in the summer, when you can attend one of the city's legendary free music festivals in downtown's Grant Park, on the shores of Lake Michigan. These open-air celebrations are generally great for families, especially those with older kids, who no longer need their hands held tightly and don't demand frequent trips to the bathroom. In fact, for preteens and young teens who feel too cool for most sight-seeing outings, attending a Chicago music festival is a great way for them to get a feel for the city's multi-culturalism, dynamism, and powerful urbanity.

Ideally, you should plan your trip around the Chicago Blues Festival, which provides the setting for the exciting conclusion of the book; it runs for four days in June. But there are several other terrific festivals in Grant Park, all of which will help bring *Yolonda's Genius* to life. Here's a rundown on each, in chronological order:

CHICAGO GOSPEL MUSIC FESTIVAL

Kicking off summer with a three-day festival at the beginning of June, this event typically showcases about forty performers, including such headliners as Lou Rawls. It has all the usual food-and-drink tents. Seek out a performance by a large gospel choir, and chances are your children will be shouting for joy.

CHICAGO BLUES FESTIVAL

Usually held in the second week of June, this is the nation's largest free blues festival, set in the blues capital of the world. Nearly seven hundred thousand people attend over the course of four days, to hear great local bar bands and such luminaries as Buddy Guy, Koko Taylor, Junior Wells, Shirley King, and zydeco master C. J. Chenier. Music is performed on several stages, but the big one is the Petrillo Music Shell, where little Andrew Blue finds fame.

TASTE OF CHICAGO

Some three and a half million people attend this ten-day festival celebrating the city's great cooking. (The festival is free, but you have to buy tickets to taste the food.) But there's much more than food: there's a 90-foot Ferris wheel, a whitewater flume ride, a family village with games, face painting, karaoke, and a video-game tent, a fabulous July 3 fireworks show accompanied by the Grant Park Orchestra, and lots of music. Headliners such as the Pointer Sisters, James Taylor, and Harry Connick Jr. perform (for free) at the Petrillo Music Shell, and another stage showcases an amazing range of local bands, playing everything from swing to reggae to polka. It's usually held at the very end of June and the first week of July.

CHICAGO COUNTRY MUSIC FESTIVAL

This two-day festival is folded into the Taste of Chicago. Stars like Willie Nelson and Dwight Yoakam play the Petrillo Music Shell; elsewhere are line-dancing lessons, bluegrass concerts, and clog-dancing performances.

VIVA CHICAGO LATIN MUSIC FESTIVAL

Held in late August, this vibrant music festival has a nice family atmosphere and is smaller than the others, typically drawing a hundred thousand people over two days. Stars like Celia Cruz and Los Tigres del Norte entertain, and in the Kids' Fun Area, there are games, clowns, jugglers, and the city's huge Jumping Jack inflatable jumping house.

CHICAGO JAZZ FESTIVAL

This is the city's oldest free music festival, and it's one of the best in the world, although it's probably the least family-friendly. The crowd is largely adult, the music tends to be less accessible to kids, and there are no kids' activities. But if your children are musicians or sophisticated music lovers, you'll want to check it out. It's held over four days in early September and has showcased many jazz greats, from Branford Marsalis to Nancy Wilson.

Besides attending a music festival, make sure to visit Yolonda's favorite place, the Harold Washington Library Center, the nation's largest municipal public library. (The book doesn't take you inside, but Yolonda loves libraries and mentions this one a couple of times.) Otherwise, just explore the Chicago attractions that interest you, and you and your family will understand why Yolonda so loves her hometown.

Names and Numbers

Chicago Summer Music
   Festivals
Mayor's Office of Special
   Events
(312) 744-3315
(800) ITS-CHGO
www.ci.chi.il.us/
   SpecialEvents/
   Festivals.html

Harold Washington Library
   Center
400 S. State St.
Chicago
(312) 747-4300
www.chipublib.org

Chicago Office of Tourism
(877) CHICAGO (244-2246)
www.ci.chi.il.us/Tourism/
Visitor centers:
Chicago Cultural Center
77 E. Randolph
   (at Michigan Ave.)
Chicago Water Works
163 E. Pearson
   (at Michigan Ave.)
Visitor centers open daily
except Thanksgiving and
Christmas.

More Storybook Travels

There's a world beyond the thirty chapters in this book. In fact, dozens more storybooks in print today have at least one real place as a setting. You may find your child's favorite book, or a favorite from your own childhood, in the collection that follows.

Betsy-Tacy, and other titles, by Maud Hart Lovelace. In this series set at the turn of the century, Betsy is a little girl living in the fictional town of Deep Valley, which is based on Lovelace's hometown of Mankato, Minnesota. Over the course of thirteen books, Betsy and Tacy venture first to the top of Hill Street (Center Street in reality), and eventually Betsy grows up and journeys as far as the big city of Milwaukee, Wisconsin.

Call of the Wild, by Jack London. London's famous story of a dog in the Far North evokes the wilderness still found around his gold-rush–era hometown of Dawson City in the Yukon, Canada.

The Cay, by Theodore Taylor. In 1942, a young white boy from the Dutch island of Curaçao is shipwrecked and blinded. He's rescued by an elderly black West Indian sailor, and together they overcome prejudices to survive on a deserted island off Costa Rica.

The Cricket in Times Square, by George Selden; illustrated by Garth Williams. Chester Cricket, like Stuart Little, is a small creature in the big city of New York. He arrives in the Times Square subway station (in a picnic basket) and makes pals with a cat, a mouse, and a boy whose parents own a newsstand.

The Farolitos of Christmas, **by Rudlfo A. Anaya; illustrated by Edward Gonzales.** Set in Northern New Mexico during World War II, this picture book shows Luz, a young Chicana, and Reina, her Native American friend, coming to the rescue when Luz's grandma is too ill to make holiday preparations.

Gentle Ben, **and other titles, by Walter Morey.** Neighbors in the Alaska Territory fear the huge brown bear named Ben, but to 13-year-old Mark, who's grieving over the death of his older brother, Ben is a loyal and lovable friend. Morey's other Alaska-based adventure titles include *Kavik the Wolf Dog* and *Scrub Dog of Alaska.*

Island Boy, **by Barbara Cooney.** A picture book for ages 4 to 8, this is the story of the youngest of twelve children living with his family on an island off of Maine.

The Islander, **by Cynthia Rylant.** Almost all of this beautiful, bittersweet book takes place on an unnamed island in British Columbia, off Vancouver, where lonely young Daniel goes to live with his grandfather and is given a gift by a mermaid.

It's Like This, Cat, **by Emily Cheney Neville.** A young teen in a more innocent time (the early 1960s) explores New York City as he grows up one summer, traveling on bike, subway, ferry, and foot from Gramercy Park and the Fulton Fish Market to Coney Island, Brooklyn, and Staten Island.

Julie of the Wolves, **by Jean Craighead George.** From Barrow, Alaska, Julie flees an arranged marriage and treks into the North Slope, thinking she will walk to Point Hope and take a ship to San Francisco. Lost, she survives in the Arctic wilderness with the help of a pack of wolves.

Lassie Come Home, by Eric Knight. Although the noble collie's year-long journey covers the hundreds of miles between northern Scotland and Yorkshire, England, it's the people and the rural life of Yorkshire that the author is passionate about.

Last of the Mohicans, by James Fenimore Cooper. Each of the Leatherstocking Tales has a different setting; much of this part of the saga takes place in and around Fort William Henry and Lake George in upstate New York.

Little Toot on the Big Canal, by Hardie Gramatky. A picture book that finds the delightfully drawn toy tugboat on the waterways of Venice, Italy.

M. C. Higgins, the Great, by Virginia Hamilton. Set in the 1970s, this National Book Award–winner is about M. C. Higgins, a boy who lives with his family in the home they've occupied since the days of his great-grandmother, who came to Ohio's Cumberland Mountains as a runaway slave.

Mary Poppins, by P. L. Travers. Although the landmark names in this cherished British classic and its sequels are fictionalized, they are recognizable London icons like Hyde Park and St. Paul's Cathedral.

My Dog Is Lost, by Ezra Jack Keats. In this book (about a Puerto Rican boy who searches for his dog on a trek through Chinatown, Harlem, and Little Italy) and other picture books, Keats celebrates the ethnic and multiethnic neighborhoods of New York.

Old Yeller, by Fred Gipson. The author, who lived in the Texas Hill Country, used the region as the setting for his classic story about a courageous dog that protects a boy and his pioneer family.

Peter Pan, by J. M. Barrie. Barrie wrote this timeless children's story in a house next to Kensington Gardens, where he later placed a statue of his memorable, magical character as a surprise for the children of London.

Pippi Longstocking, by **Astrid Lindgren.** Tommy and Annika, two children living in Sweden, are amazed and thrilled when the outrageous, and outrageously strong, Pippi comes to live next door to them. In a sequel, they go with her to the South Seas.

Roll of Thunder, Hear My Cry, by **Mildred D. Taylor.** The Logans have owned their 400 acres of farmland in Jefferson Davis County, Mississippi, since 1918, and during one year in the 1930s—a year when the injustices of racism hit her family hard—young Cassie learns why her parents will do anything to keep their land.

Strawberry Girl, by **Lois Lenski.** This Newbery winner follows 10-year-old Birdie Boyer, who moves with her family to a farm in the Florida backwoods in the '30s.

Strega Nona, by **Tomie DePaola.** The Caldecott Award–winning illustrations in this well-loved picture book show Strega Nona and Big Anthony in a village in Calabria, Italy.

Uptown, by **Brian Collier.** Published in the year 2000 by an artist who also directs mural programs in New York City, this picture book for ages 4 to 8 shows Harlem from a young resident's point of view, with photo and paint collages of churchgoers, shoppers, landmark buildings, cafés, and barbershops.

The Wonderful Adventures of Nils, by **Selma Lagerlof.** A national hero in Sweden (where he's depicted on the 10-kroner bill), Nils is a boy who travels around that country on the back of a flying goose. It was written by the first woman to win the Nobel prize for literature.

Index of Titles

This is a comprehensive list of all books mentioned in *Storybook Travels*, ranging from titles covered in entire chapters to titles mentioned briefly in the text.

Illustration Credits

The Adventures of Pinocchio: Illustration from Parco di Pinocchio. Copyright and trademark by Fondazione Nazionale Carlo Collodi.

And Now Miguel: Illustration copyright © 1953 Jean Charlot. Used by permission of HarperCollins Publishers.

A Bear Called Paddington: Illustration from *A Bear Called Paddington* by Michael Bond, illustrated by Peggy Fortnum. Copyright © 1958, renewed 1986 by Michael Bond. Reprinted by permission of Houghton Mifflin Company. All rights reserved.

Eloise: Illustration reprinted with the permission of Simon & Schuster Books for Young Readers, an imprint of Simon & Schuster Children's Publishing Division, from *The Absolutely Essential Eloise* by Kay Thompson. Drawings by Hilary Knight. Copyright © 1955 by Kay Thompson; copyright renewed 1983 by Kay Thompson.

Hill of Fire: Illustration copyright © 1971 by Joan Sandin. Used by permission of HarperCollins Publishers.

Linnea in Monet's Garden: Illustration from *Linnea in Monet's Garden* by Christina Bjork and Lena Anderson. Copyright © 1987 by Christina Bjork and Lena Anderson. Reprinted by permission of Farrar, Straus & Giroux, LLC.

Little House on the Prairie: Picture copyright © 1953 Garth Williams. Used by permission of HarperCollins Publishers.

The Little Red Lighthouse and the Great Gray Bridge: Illustration from *The Little Red Lighthouse and the Great Gray Bridge* by Hildegarde H. Swift and Lynd Ward, copyright

About the Authors

COLLEEN DUNN BATES and SUSAN LATEMPA have been colleagues for longer than they've been mothers, although their early professional association revolved around sophisticated dining, not storybooks. They met at *L.A. Style* magazine, where Bates was the restaurant critic and LaTempa her editor. In the years since, they have each worked as editors, magazine journalists, and book authors (Bates is the author of *The Eclectic Gourmet Guide to Los Angeles*, LaTempa is a co-author of the *Summer Garden Cookbook*). Later, they found themselves on parallel paths when both began to focus on travel writing. After swapping stories and tips as they journeyed with their children, husbands, extended family, and friends, the two drew upon a decade of family-travel adventures to collaborate on *The Unofficial Guide to California with Kids* (IDG), now in its third edition. Not content to stay at home with the kids, they then dreamed up *Storybook Travels* and have been on the road ever since.